A Grammar of the Irish Language

Joyce, P. W. (Patrick Weston)

Copyright © BiblioLife, LLC

This historical reproduction is part of a unique project that provides opportunities for readers, educators and researchers by bringing hard-to-find original publications back into print at reasonable prices. Because this and other works are culturally important, we have made them available as part of our commitment to protecting, preserving and promoting the world's literature. These books are in the "public domain" and were digitized and made available in cooperation with libraries, archives, and open source initiatives around the world dedicated to this important mission.

We believe that when we undertake the difficult task of re-creating these works as attractive, readable and affordable books, we further the goal of sharing these works with a global audience, and preserving a vanishing wealth of human knowledge.

Many historical books were originally published in small fonts, which can make them very difficult to read. Accordingly, in order to improve the reading experience of these books, we have created "enlarged print" versions of our books. Because of font size variation in the original books, some of these may not technically qualify as "large print" books, as that term is generally defined; however, we believe these versions provide an overall improved reading experience for many.

A GRAMMAR

OF THE

IRISH LANGUAGE

BY

P. W. JOYCE, LL.D., T.C.D., M.R.I.A.,
ONE OF THE PROFESSORS IN THE TRAINING DEPARTMENT OF THE
COMMISSIONERS OF NATIONAL EDUCATION, IRELAND.

DUBLIN
M. H. GILL AND SON
1896.

WORKS BY P. W. JOYCE, LL.D.

1. A Short History of Ireland from the Earliest Times to 1608; 565 pages; cloth. 10*s.* 6*d*
2. A Concise History of Ireland from the Earliest Times to 1837; 312 pages; Fifth Ed.; cloth, 2*s.*
3. Outlines of the History of Ireland from the Earliest Times to 1837; 126 pages; cloth, 9*d.*
4. The Origin and History of Irish Names of Places. Sixth Ed.; (in two volumes); 5*s.* each.
5. Irish Local Names Explained, 1*s.*
6. Old Celtic Romances; Translated from the Gaelic. Second Ed.; cloth, 3*s.* 6*d.*
7. A Grammar of the Irish Language, 1*s.*
8. "Keating" for Students of Gaelic. With Translation and Notes; wrapper, 1*s.* 4*d.*; cloth, 2*s.*
9. Ancient Irish Music; 100 Irish Airs. With Popular Songs; wrapper, 1*s.* 6*d.*; cloth, 3*s.*
10. The Geography of the Counties of Ireland. With a General Description of the Country, 3*s.* 6*d.*
11. A Hand-Book of School Management and Methods of Teaching. Fifteenth Ed.; 3*s.* 6*d.*
12. A Concise History of England to A.D. 1815, 1*s.*
13. A Concise History of Rome to the Death of Sulla, 1*s.* 6*d.*
14. English Composition for the Use of Schools. Fifth Ed.; 6*d.*

TO BE HAD FROM

M. H. GILL & SON, DUBLIN.

PREFACE.

Though this text-book is small, it comprises, I believe, everything necessary—so far as grammar is concerned—for a student of modern Irish. I have not treated at all of the ancient forms of the language; and I have excluded everything in the shape of dissertation: the grammar of the modern Irish language, and no more, is here set forth in words as few and simple as possible.

I have not suggested any changes either in spelling or in grammatical forms, or attempted innovation of any kind: this is a grammar of the language as it actually exists in the works of our best writers.

All the illustrative examples are quotations from standard Irish writings; but though I retain the references, I have not given them in the grammar, as they would encumber the book, and impede, rather than facilitate the learner. I may mention here, however, that the works from which the examples are chiefly taken, are, those of Keating, the publications of the Ossianic Society, "The Three Sorrowful Stories of Erin" (viz., "The Fate of the Children of Usna," "The Fate of the Children of Lir," and "The Fate of the Children of Turenn"), and occasionally the "Annals of the Four Masters." The language of the various works published by the Archæological and Celtic Societies is generally too antiquated to be quoted in a grammar of modern Irish.

I have all through given word-for-word translations of the examples; free translations would have been more pleasant to read, but would have added considerably to the learner's difficulty.

In the last Part—"Idioms"—I have given a popular rather than a scientific explanation of the principal idioms of the language. Nothing like this is to be found in any other Irish Grammar; and I believe that the learner who masters it will be saved much labour and perplexity.

There are several other Irish Grammars, but none low enough in price to be within reach of the many. Whoever wishes to study the Irish language in its ancient as well as in its modern forms, must procure O'Donovan's Grammar; without this great work no one can attain a thorough knowledge of the language. I may also mention "The College Irish Grammar," by the Rev. Ulick J. Canon Bourke, in which there is a great amount of miscellaneous information on the language, proverbs, and popular literature of Ireland.

The labours of the Society for the Preservation of the Irish Language have lately given a great impetus to Celtic studies. The Society has produced two admirable little elementary books (the First and Second Irish Books) and are about to bring out a third all drawn up by the members themselves on the plan of the elementary works of Smith, Arnold, Ahn, &c. But the want of a very cheap and simple text-book on Irish Grammar has been much felt; and this Grammar has been written to supply the want. I have written it with the cognisance of the Council of the Society, of which I am myself a member. It was at first intended that the name of the Society should appear on the title-page along with my own name, and a resolution to that effect was passed by the Council. But I found some difficulty as to the exact words, and I have accordingly contented myself with mentioning the matter here.

I acknowledge with thanks that I have received valuable assistance from several gentlemen of the Society, who read every word of my proofs, suggesting various corrections, alterations, and improvements. One member in particular, Mr. John Fleming of Rathgormuck, in the county Waterford, read all my manuscript in the first instance, and all the proof-sheets afterwards. Mr. Fleming's assistance was invaluable to me, for he possesses an intimate knowledge of modern Irish Grammar, language, and literature, and what is still better, much sound sense and clear critical judgment.

Dublin, November, 1878.

CONTENTS.

PART I.

ORTHOGRAPHY.

	PAGE
CHAPTER I.—SOUNDS	1
I. Letters	1
II. Diphthongs	4
III. Triphthongs	6
IV. Various Sounds	6
CHAPTER II.—LETTER CHANGES	8
I. Aspiration	8
II. Rules for Aspiration	9
III. Eclipsis	10
IV. Rules for Eclipsis	11
V. Caol le caol aᵹur leaṫan le leaṫan	13
VI. Syncope	14

PART II.

ETYMOLOGY.

CHAPTER I.—THE ARTICLE	16
I. Change of form in the Article	16
II. Changes produced by the Article	17
Singular	17
Plural	18

CONTENTS.

	PAGE
CHAPTER II.—THE NOUN	18
I. Gender	18
Masculine	19
Feminine	19
II. Declensions	20
Cases	20
First Declension	21
Second Declension	23
Third Declension	25
Fourth Declension	27
Fifth Declension	28
Irregular Declension	28
Declension of the Article with the Noun	30
CHAPTER III.—THE ADJECTIVE	32
I. Declension of Adjectives	32
First Declension	32
Second Declension	33
Third Declension	33
Fourth Declension	34
II. Declension of the Article and Adjective with the Noun	34
III. Comparison of Adjectives	35
Irregular Comparison	36
IV. Numeral Adjectives	37
CHAPTER IV.—THE PRONOUN	39
I. Personal Pronouns	39
Declension of Personal Pronouns	40
Personal Pronouns compounded with Prepositions	41
II. Possessive Pronouns	44
Possessive Pronouns compounded with Prepositions	45
III. Relative Pronouns	46
IV. Demonstrative Pronouns	47
V. Interrogative Pronouns	47
VI. Indefinite Pronouns	47

CONTENTS.

	PAGE
CHAPTER V.—THE VERB	48
I. Persons: Synthetic and Analytic forms	48
II. Tenses	50
III. Moods and Voices	51
IV. Conjugation of the regular Verb buail	52
IV. Relative form of the Verb	55
V. Formation and uses of the moods and tenses of Regular Verbs	56
VI. Verbs in uiġ, il, in, iṗ, ir	62
Paradigm of the regular Verb meall	64
Paradigm of the regular Verb áṗḃuiġ	65
VII. Irregular Verbs	66
1. Táim, I am	66
2. Iṗ, it is	71
3. Ḃeiṗim, I give	73
4. Beiṗim, I bear	74
5. Ċím, I see	75
6. Cluinim, I hear	76
7. Ḋéanaim, I do	77
8. Ġním or ním, I do	78
9. Ḋeiṗim, I say	78
10. Ḟaġaim or ġeiḃim, I find	80
11. Iṫim, I eat	81
12. Riġim, I reach	81
13. Ṫéiḋim, I go	82
14. Tiġim, I come	83
Other Defective Verbs	84
CHAPTER VI.—ADVERBS, PREPOSITIONS, CONJUNCTIONS, INTERJECTIONS	85
I. Adverbs	85
II. Prepositions	87
III. Conjunctions	89
IV. Interjections	90
CHAPTER VII.—PREFIXES AND AFFIXES	91
I. Prefixes	91
II. Affixes or terminations	93

CONTENTS.

PART III.

SYNTAX.

	PAGE
CHAPTER I.—NOUNS	95
CHAPTER II.—THE ARTICLE AND NOUN	98
CHAPTER III.—THE ADJECTIVE AND NOUN	100
Agreement and collocation of the Adjective and Noun	100
CHAPTER IV.—NUMERAL ADJECTIVES	104
CHAPTER V.—THE PRONOUN	105
I. Personal Pronouns	105
II. Possessive Pronouns	106
III. Relative Pronouns	107
IV. Demonstrative Pronouns	109
V. Interrogative and Indefinite Pronouns	109
CHAPTER VI.—THE VERB	110
CHAPTER VII.—PREPOSITIONS	113

PART IV.

IDIOMS.

Explanation and illustration of forty-three Idioms of the Irish Language	116

APPENDIX.

Additional examples of declensions of Nouns	136

SCHOOL IRISH GRAMMAR.

PART I.

ORTHOGRAPHY.

CHAPTER I.

SOUNDS.

I. LETTERS.

1. The Irish alphabet consists of eighteen letters, of which thirteen are consonants and five are vowels.

2. The five vowels are a, e, ı, o, u; of which a, o, u are broad, and e, ı are slender.

3. Each consonant (with the exceptions mentioned below) has a broad and a slender sound. When a consonant comes immediately after or before a broad vowel, it has its broad sound: when it comes after or before a slender vowel, it has its slender sound. But this does not apply to b, ꝑ, h, m, p, each of which has one sound only, whether joined with a broad vowel or a slender vowel.

4. Vowels are either long or short. A long vowel is usually marked by an accent; as bán, white: a short vowel has no mark; as mac, a son.

5. The Irish vowels, like the English, have an obscure sound in unaccented syllables, of which it is not necessary to take further notice here.

6. The following are the usual sounds of the Irish letters, so far as they can be represented by English letters.

7. Those marked with asterisks are only imperfectly represented in sound by the corresponding English letters: those not so marked are represented perfectly or very nearly so.

8. The sounds of the marked letters must be learned by ear: it is hardly possible to give in writing such a description of them as would enable a learner to utter them.

9. C is equal to *k*, yet when it comes before the diphthong ao or the triphthong aoi, beginners find it very hard to sound it: caol (narrow) is neither *kail* or *quail*, but something between: caoin (gentle) is neither *keen* or *queen*, but something between.

10. So also with ʒ, which (broad and slender) is equal to *g* in *got* and *get:* yet ʒaol is hard for a beginner to utter, being neither *gail* nor *gwail*, but something between.

11. The Irish broad ɒ and c bear the same relation to each other as the English *d* and *t;* that is, the first in each case is flat or soft, and the second sharp or hard. English *d* and *t* are sounded by placing the tip of the tongue against the roof of the mouth: Irish ɒ and c by placing the top of the tongue against the upper front teeth. Irish ɒ and c may be described in another way: the two sounds of *th* in *those* and *thumb* are both *continuous*, the first flat, the second sharp. Now the two *explosive* sounds corresponding to these two continuous sounds (i.e., with the tongue in the same position), are exactly the Irish ɒ and c.

12. Broad l and n are sounded by placing the top of the tongue (not against the roof of the mouth as in case of English *l* and *n* but) against the upper front teeth. Irish ɒ and c are to English *d* and *t* as Irish l or n to English *l* or *n*.

13. Slender p is the most difficult of all the Irish consonantal sounds: and learners, unless they have acquired it in youth, often fail to articulate it correctly, though the teacher may sound it over and over again for their imitation.

14. As h represents a mere breathing or aspiration and not an articulate sound, and as it never begins a word, some writers exclude it from the letters, thus making seventeen instead of eighteen, as given here.

TABLE OF SOUNDS.

Letters.		Vowel long or short.	Consonant broad or slender.	Irish sounds.	Corresponding English sounds.
Irish.	Eng.				
ɑ	a	a	long	..	lán	lawn, ball
			short	..	mac	bat or what
ḃ	ḃ	b	..	..	ball	ban
c	c	c	..	broad	cab	cob
			..	slender	cin	king
ḋ	ḋ	d	..	broad	dall	those
			..	slender	dian	cordial
e	e	e	long	..	mé	date
			short	..		met
ḟ	f	f	..	..	finn	fin
ġ	ġ	g	..	broad	gort	got
			..	slender	geir	get, gimlet
h	h	h	..	..	a h-anam	hammer
i	i	i	long	..	mín	seen
			short	..	min	pin
l	l	l	..	broad	lón	lone
			..	slender	pile	vermilion
ṁ	m	m	..	..	mil	mill
N	n	n	..	broad	nór	none
			..	slender	nead	new
o	o	o	long	..	món	more
			short	..	dor	love, run
ṗ	p	p	..	..	poc	pore
R	r	r	..	broad	ród	road
			..	slender	cuir	clarion
ṡ	s	s	..	broad	rona	son
			..	slender	rín	sheen
ṫ	t	t	..	broad	tom	thumb
			..	slender	teine	courteous
u	u	u	long	...	múr	moor, rude
			short	...	muc	put, bull

15. The following are the native names of the Irish letters, but they need not be used by the learner. All or most of them are the names of trees. Ailm, *a*; beiṫ, *b*; coll, *c*; dair, *d*; eaḋa, *e*; fearn, *f*; gort, *g*; uaṫ, *h*; ioġa, *i*; luir, *l*; muin, *m*; nuin, *n*; oir or onn, *o*; peiṫ-boġ, *p*; ruir, *r*; ruil, *s*; teine, *t*; úr, *u*.

II. DIPHTHONGS.

1. There are thirteen diphthongs in the Irish language—viz., ae, ao, eu, ia, ua, ai, ea, ei, eo, io, iu, oi, ui; of which the first five are always long, and the remaining eight are sometimes long and sometimes short.

2. The following are the sounds of the five long diphthongs :—

3. ae sounds like *ay* in *slay;* as ρae, the moon, pronounced *ray.*

4. ao, in the southern half of Ireland, sounds nearly like *way*, and in the west and north-west somewhat like *we*. Thus maoρ, a steward, is pronounced like *mwair* in the south, and like *mweer* in the west and north-west.

5. eu like *ai* in *lair;* as in ρeuρ, grass, pronounced *fair.*

6. ia like *ee* in *beer;* as in ciaρ, dark-coloured, pronounced *keer.*

7. ua nearly like *oe* in *doer;* as in luan, Monday, pronounced *loo-an.*

8. The following are the sounds of the eight diphthongs that are sometimes long and sometimes short. When these diphthongs are long there is an accent over one of the vowels: when short there is no accent.

9. ái long has an accent over the a, and sounds something like the *awi* in *drawing;* as in cáin, tribute, pronounced *caw-in.*

ai short is sounded something like the *a* in *valiant* or the *o* in *collier;* as in maiċ, good, whose sound is very nearly represented by *moh.*

In Ulster, ai short is pronounced like short *e* in *bell:* as in aiρioc, restitution, which is pronounced *eshoc* in the north, and *ashoc* in the south and west.

10. éa long has an accent over the e, and sounds

like *ea* in *bear;* thus méaꞃ, a finger, is pronounced *mare*.

ea short sounds like *ea* in *heart* (but shorter); as in ꞅeaꞃ, knowledge, pronounced *fass*.

11. éı long has an accent over the e, and sounds like *ei* in *rein;* as ꞅéım, a course, pronounced *raim*.

eı short, like *e* in *sell;* as in ceıꞃ, a basket, sounded like *kesh*.

12. eó long has an accent over the o, and is sounded nearly like long English *o* with a slight sound of *y* before it; as in ceól, music, which will be correctly pronounced if a *k* sound is put before the word *yole*.

eo short, nearly like *u* in *shut*, with *y* before it; as in ḃeoċ, drink.

Note.—This diphthong is short in only a very few words.

13. ío long has an accent over the ı, and sounds very like *ea* in *hear;* as in ꞅíon, wine, pronounced *feen* or *fee-on*.

ıo short, nearly like short *i;* as in mıoꞃꞃ, myrrh, which has nearly the same sound as the first syllable of *mirror*.

14. ıú long has an accent over the u, and has the same sound as the diphthongal English *u* in *tune;* as in ꞅıú, worthy, which is sounded exactly like *few*.

ıu short is sounded like the *u* in *put*, with a *y* before it; as in ꞅlıuċ, wet.

15. óı long has an accent over the o, and is sounded like the *owi* in *owing;* as in ꞃóıl, a while, pronounced *fō-il*.

oı short like the *o* in *love*, with a very short *i* at the end; as in coıl, the will.

16. úı long, with an accent over the u, is sounded like *ooi* in *cooing;* as ꞅúıl, the eye, pronounced *soo-il*.

uí long, with an accent over the ı, has nearly the same sound as *we;* as in buíoe, yellow, which is pronounced *bwee.*

uı short is like the *ui* in *quill;* as in puıpeóʒ, a lark, pronounced *fwishoge.*

III. TRIPHTHONGS.

1. There are commonly reckoned five triphthongs, which are always long:—aoı, eoı, ıaı, ıuı, uaı.

2. Aoı is sounded very like *we,* as in maoın, wealth, pronounced *mween.*

3. Eoı is sounded like the *yoi* in the combination *yō-ing;* as in peoıl, flesh, which will be correctly pronounced if the sound of *f* is put before the combination *yō-il.*

4. ıaı is sounded like *eei* in *seeing;* as lıaıʒ, a physician.

5. ıuı like the *ewi* in *mewing;* as cıuın, gentle.

6. Uaı like *ooi* in *cooing;* as buaıl, strike, which is sounded *boo-il.*

7. The preceding attempts to represent the sounds of the diphthongs and triphthongs are in many cases mere approximations. The student must hear them pronounced, and in no other way is it possible to learn to sound them correctly.

IV. VARIOUS SOUNDS.

1. A and o before m, nn, ll, or nʒ, in monosyllables, and often before nc and nc, are sounded in Munster like the *ou* in *foul;* as cam, crooked, and coll, hazel, pronounced *cowm* and *cowl;* and ʒleanncán, a small glen, pronounced *glounthaun:* and o before ƀ and ʒ̇ has often the same sound; as poʒlaım, learning, pronounced *fowlim.*

2. Aȯ and aʒ̇ are often sounded like long English *i* in *fine;* as paȯaıc, sight, pronounced *y-ark;* laḃap, a fork, pronounced *lyre;* maṁ, a breach, pronounced *mime.*

3. The termination aḃ is pronounced in Connaught nearly the same as *oo:* thus bualaḃ, striking, is pronounced *booloo* in Connaught, but *boola* in Munster.

4. In the combination ḃl, the ḃ is silent, and the whole is sounded like l or ll; as coḃlaḃ, sleep, pronounced *culla.*

5. In the combination ln, the *n* is silent, and the whole is sounded like l or ll; as colna, of a body, pronounced *culla.*

6. In the combination ḃn, the ḃ is silent, and the whole is sounded the same as n or nn; as céaḃna, the same, pronounced *kaina.*

7. Final e is never entirely silent in Irish as it is in English; thus mine, smoothness, is pronounced *meena.* In some situations it is very nearly silent in the modern language; as in cpoiḃe, a heart, pronounced *cree.*

8. There are some Irish consonants which, when they come together in a word, do not coalesce in sound, so that when they are uttered, a *very* short obscure vowel sound is heard between them.

This generally occurs in the case of two liquids, or a liquid and a mute. Thus lopg, a track, is pronounced so as to seem, to an ear accustomed to English, a word of two syllables; not *lurg* but *lurrug.* ḃealḃ, a shape, is sounded, not *dalv,* but *dallav;* pcapb, bitter, is sounded *sharrav;* bopb, proud, is pronounced *burrub;* colg, a sword, *cullug,* and so on. In Irish prosody, however, such words as these count as only one syllable.

In the English language no such difficulty exists in regard to most of these letters; they coalesce perfectly in sound, so that each of the above words would be a pure monosyllable.

CHAPTER II.

LETTER CHANGES.

I. ASPIRATION.

1. The term "aspiration" is used to express a certain change of sound suffered by some of the Irish consonants under certain grammatical conditions.

2. It is impossible to give a definition of aspiration that will correctly describe all the cases, inasmuch as the changes of sound vary in kind with the several consonants. In most cases the change caused by aspiration is one from an *explosive* to a *continuous* sound.

3. There are nine consonants which can be aspirated, namely, b, c, ᴅ, p, ᵹ, m, p, ɼ, τ; these are called mutable or aspirable consonants; the others are called immutable. The aspiration is denoted either by placing a point over the consonant, as ċ; or by placing h after it, as ch.

4. The following are the sounds of the aspirated consonants so far as they can be represented by English letters.

5. bh or ḃ is sounded sometimes like *v* and sometimes like *w*, and it often has a sound something between both; as a ḃean, his wife, pronounced *a van;* ᵹaḃal, a fork, pronounced *gowal*.

6. Ch broad has a guttural sound which is not represented in English; but it is heard in the pronunciation of the word *lough*, Irish loċ, a lake.

Ch slender (i.e. joined with a slender vowel) has a less guttural sound than ċ broad; as miċiall, folly, in which the ċ sound is only a little more guttural than *h* in *mee-heel*.

7. Ḋh and ġ have the same sound. When slender, they are sounded like initial *y* in English; as a ġean, his love, pronounced *a yan*. Ḋh and ġ broad have a guttural sound which cannot be represented by English letters, though it is something like initial *y* or initial *w*; it stands to the guttural sound of broad ċ in the relation of flat to hard. Both these aspirated letters are silent at the end of a word; as ꝼιαḋ, a deer, pronounced *fee-a*.

But in south Munster the final ġ is fully sounded, like *g* in *fig*: as Coɼcaιġ (dative of Coɼcaċ, Cork), pronounced *curkig* in Munster, but *curkee* elsewhere.

8. Fh is always silent; thus a ꝼιoꞃ, his knowledge, is pronounced *a iss*; an ꝼeaḋóġ, the plover, pronounced *an addoge*.

9. Mh is very nearly the same as ḃ, viz., like *v* or *w*; as a ṁιaꞃ, his dish, pronounced *a vee-as*.

10. Ph has the sound of *f*, as a ꝼιan, his pain, pronounced *a fee-an*.

11. Sh and ṫ are the same as *h*; as a ꞅál, his heel, pronounced *a haul*; a ṫoḃaꞃ, his well, pronounced *a hubber*.

II. RULES FOR ASPIRATION.*

1. The possessive pronouns mo, my; do, thy; and a, his, aspirate the first consonant of the next word: as mo ḃó, my cow; do ċeann, thy head; a ġoꞃτ, his garden.

2. The article aspirates in the singular feminine nominative and accusative;† as an ḃean, the woman. (See also p. 18, Par. 6, and p. 31.)

3. The article aspirates in the genitive singular masculine; as an ġuιꞃτ, of the garden.

---

* These rules cannot be fully understood without a knowledge of Etymology. It must be borne in mind that they apply only to the aspirable or mutable consonants.

† Irish nouns have no inflection for the accusative (or objective) case; but it is often convenient to speak of nouns in the accusative, by which is meant the case where the noun is the object of a transitive verb, or sometimes of a preposition.

NOTE.—This rule and the preceding do not apply to the letter ꞃ. (See also p. 18, Par. 6, and p. 31.)

4. In compound words, the initial consonant of the second word of the compound is aspirated (with a few exceptions): thus from ceann, a head, and bꞃaꞇ, a garment, is formed ceannḃꞃaꞇ, head-garment or canopy. (See also p. 34, Par. 2.)

5. The interjections a and O, as signs of the vocative case, aspirate; as a ḟiꞃ, O man.

6. An adjective agreeing with a noun has its initial consonant aspirated when the noun is nominative singular feminine, or genitive singular masculine, or vocative singular of both genders; and, according to O'Donovan, in the nominative plural masculine, when the noun ends in a consonant; as bó ḃán, a white cow; caiꞇ ḃáin, of a white cat; a ḟiꞃ ṁóiꞃ, O great man; a ḃean ḟeiṅ, O mild woman; capaill ḃána, white horses. (ꝺ and ꞇ are sometimes excepted: see p. 34.)

7. The initial consonant of a verb is aspirated (1) in the infinitive mood by the particles ꝺo and a; as ꝺo ḋéanaḋ or a ḋéanaḋ, to do: (2), in the simple past tense, active voice; as ꝺo ḟeaꞃ ꞃé, he stood: (3) by the particles ní, not, and má, if: as ní ḃeiḋ ꞃí, she will not be; má ḟeaꞃann ꞃé, if he stands; (4), by the relative a, who, (expressed or understood); as an ꞇé a ḃuailcaꞃ the person who strikes. (See also pp. 58 and 60.)

8. The simple prepositions, with some exceptions, aspirate the initial consonants of nouns: as aiꞃ ḃáꞃꞃ, on top; ꝺo ṁullaċ, to a summit; ꝼaoi ġean, under affection.

III. ECLIPSIS.

1. A consonant is said to be eclipsed, or to suffer eclipsis, when its sound is suppressed, and the sound of another consonant which is prefixed to it, substituted: thus in n-ꝺán, ꝺ is eclipsed by n

CHAP. II.]   LETTER CHANGES.   11

and the whole word is pronounced *nawn*, whereas ᴅán is pronounced *dawn*. It is only at the beginning of words that consonants are eclipsed.

2. The following eight consonants can be eclipsed:—b, c, ᴅ, ꝑ, ꙅ, p, ꞃ, ꞇ; the others cannot. Between the eclipsing and the eclipsed letter there is usually placed a hyphen, as m-bárᴅ; but often they are put together without any separating mark, as bpopꞇ. Sometimes eclipsis is denoted by the doubling of the eclipsed letter; thus a ꞇꞇaꝑb is the same as a ᴅ-ꞇaꝑb, their bull.

3. Each consonant has an eclipsing letter of its own.

4. b is eclipsed by m; as a m-bárᴅ, their bard, pronounced *a mawrd*.

5. C is eclipsed by ꙅ: as a ꙅ-coll, their hazel, pronounced *a gowl* or *a gull*.

6. ᴅ by n; as a n-ᴅop, their bush, pronounced *a nuss*.

7. ꝑ by b (which itself sounds like *v* or *w*); as a b-ꝑeaꞃann, their land, pronounced *a varran*.

8. ꙅ is eclipsed by n. But this is not a true eclipsis, for the resulting sound is not that of n, but the sound of English *ng:* thus a nꙅiolla, their servant, is pronounced *ang-illa*.

9. p is eclipsed by b; as a b-pian, their pain, pronounced *a bee-an*.

10. S is eclipsed by ꞇ, as in an ꞇ-púil, the eye, pronounced *an too-il*.

11. ꞇ is eclipsed by ᴅ; as a ᴅ-ꞇál, their adze, pronounced *a dawl*.

IV. RULES FOR ECLIPSIS.*

1. The possessive pronouns plural—áꞃ, our.

* These rules apply of course only to those consonants that can be eclipsed. The rules for eclipsis, like those for aspiration, suppose a knowledge of Etymology.

bup, your; a, their; eclipse the initial consonant of the next word; as áp b-tıżeapna, our Lord; bup ʒ-cpann, your tree; a b-páıpc, their field.*

2. The article eclipses the initial consonant of nouns in the genitive plural; as teać na m-bápb, the house of the bards; ʒopt na ʒ-capall, the field of the horses.

3. When a simple preposition is followed by the article and a noun in the singular number, the initial consonant of the noun is generally eclipsed; as aıp an m-bópb, on the table; ó'n b-paıpʒe, from the sea. (See p. 31; see also Syntax.)

4. The initial consonant of a verb is eclipsed after the interrogative particles a, an, cá, nać; also after ʒo, that; muna, unless; ıap, after; bá, if; and after the relative a preceded by a preposition; as a m-beıpcann pe? Does he bear? an m-buaılcann tú? Dost thou strike? cá b-puıl pí? Where is she? nać b-tuıʒeann tu? Dost thou not understand? ʒo m-beannaıʒe Ʋıa ɓuıt, may God bless thee; muna b-tuıtpıp, unless thou shalt fall; bá n-beappaınn, if I would say; an típ ann a b-taınıc pıab, the country into which they came.

5. When a noun beginning with p is preceded by the article, the p is eclipsed when the noun is nominative feminine, or genitive masculine, and generally in the dative of both genders, as an t-paoıppe (fem.), the freedom; ʒopt an t-paʒaıpt, the field of the priest; aıp an t-paoʒal, or ap an paoʒal, in the world. But if the p is followed by b, c, b, ʒ. m, p, or t, it is not eclipsed; as ʒleann an pmóıl, the valley of the thrush; loć an pcáıl, the lake of the champion. (See pp. 30 and 31.)

* Rules 1, 2, 3, 4, do not apply to p. See for this letter Rule 5.

6. The following rule is usually given with the rules for eclipsis :—

When a word begins with a vowel, the letter n is generally prefixed in all cases where an initial consonant (except ꞅ) would be eclipsed ; as a n-aꞃán, their bread ; loċ na n-éan, the lake of the birds.*

V. Caol le caol aᵹuꞅ leaṫan le leaṫan, OR SLENDER WITH SLENDER AND BROAD WITH BROAD.†

1. If a consonant or any combination of consonants comes between two vowels, they must be either both slender or both broad ; thus in ꞅolaꞅ, light, the o and the a are both broad vowels ; and in ṫinneaꞅ, sickness, the ı and the e are both slender vowels. But such combinations as ꞅolıꞅ and ṫinnaꞅ are not allowable, because the o and the ı in the first case, and the ı and the a in the second case, are one of them broad and the other slender.

2. In compliance with this rule, when two words, or a word and a syllable, are joined together, so that in the resulting word a consonant or consonantal combination would fall between two vowels, one of them broad and the other slender, then either the broad vowel must be made slender or the slender one broad, to bring them to an agreement.

3. Sometimes the broad vowel is changed to make it agree with the slender vowel ; sometimes the slender vowel is made broad to agree with the broad vowel ; sometimes it is the vowel before the consonant that is changed ; sometimes the change is made in the vowel after the consonant. A prefix is generally changed to suit the word it is joined to, not the reverse ; thus when cóṁ is prefixed to ꞅeaꞅaṁ, standing, the word is cóiṁꞅeaꞅaṁ, competition, not cóṁꞅaꞅaṁ.

---

* For a very detailed and clear statement of the laws of aspiration and eclipsis, see the Second Irish Book by the Society for the preservation of the Irish Language.

† This rule is very generally, but not universally, followed in the Irish language.

4. Changing a broad vowel to a slender is called in Irish caoluġaḋ (i.e., making slender, from caol, slender), and in English *attenuation*; changing from slender to broad is called in Irish leaṫnuġaḋ (i.e., making broad, from leaṫan, broad).

5. Attenuation takes place chiefly in two ways:—first by putting a slender vowel between the broad vowel and the consonant, as when ball, a spot, is changed to baill, spots; or when pá is postfixed to buail, and the resulting word is buailpeá, not buailpá: secondly, by removing the broad vowel which precedes or follows the consonant, and putting a slender vowel in its place; as when ceann, a head, is changed to cinn, of a head.

6. In like manner "making broad" takes place chiefly in two ways, which are the reverse of the two preceding.

7. The following examples will illustrate the preceding rules and remarks:—

8. When the future termination paḋ is added to buail, the resulting word is not buailpaḋ, but buailpeaḋ, I shall strike.

9. When the infinitive termination aḋ is added to buail, the resulting word is not buailaḋ but bualaḋ.

10. When mór, great, is prefixed to cion, love, the compound is not mórcion but móircion, great love.

11. When ceann, head, is prefixed to litir, a letter, the compound is not ceannlitir but cinnlitir, a head-letter or capital letter. (This is a case of irregular attenuation.)

12. When the diminutive termination óg is added to cuil, the resulting word is not cuilóg but cuileóg, a fly.

13. When e is added to orḋóg, a thumb, to inflect it for the genitive, the word is not orḋóge but orḋóige, of a thumb.

14. When the diminutive termination ín is added to capall, a horse, the whole word is not capallín but capaillín.

VI. SYNCOPE.

1. Syncope, or the omission of one or more letters from the body of a word, is very common in Irish.

2. When a short vowel occurs between a liquid (l, n, r, or ŗ) and a mute, or between two liquids, the word is often syncopated when it is lengthened either by grammatical inflection or otherwise.

CHAP. II.] LETTER CHANGES. 15

3. The syncope generally consists in the omission of the short vowel; but this change often involves others in accordance with the rule caol le caol &c.; and is often also accompanied by some slight consonantal changes.

4. The following examples exhibit the chief types of syncope.

5. Lánaṁa, a married couple; plural lánaṁna, contracted from lánaṁana.

6. Lapaıp, a flame; plural lappaċa, contracted from lapapaċa.

7. Pocal, a word; poclóıp, a dictionary, contracted from pocalóıp.

8. Saıbıp, rich; comparative paıbpe, contracted from paıbıpe.

9. Caċaıp, a city; genitive caċpaċ, contracted from caċapaċ.

10. Plaıċeaṁaıl, princely; comparative plaıċeaṁla, contracted from plaıċeaṁala.

11. Colann, the body, genitive colna, (sometimes colla), contracted from colanna.

12. Capa, genitive capaɒ: the plural is formed by adding e to this, which syncopates the second a: this would make capɒe, which again, in accordance with the rule caol le caol &c., is made caıpɒe.

13. Uapal, noble, becomes uaıple in the comparative, by a process exactly similar to the last.

14. Pollup, evident, becomes poıllpe in the comparative in a similar way.

15. Aɒann, a river: the plural is formed by adding e; this causes syncope of the second a and the omission of one n, which would make the plural aɒne; and this again becomes aıɒne, by the rule caol le caol &c.

16. Labaıp, speak (imperative mood); labpaım, I speak, contracted from labapaım,

PART II.
ETYMOLOGY.

1. There are nine parts of speech in Irish, which are the same as those in English.

CHAPTER I.
THE ARTICLE.
I. CHANGE OF FORM IN THE ARTICLE.

1. The Irish language has one article, an, which has the same meaning as the English definite article *the*.

2. The article changes its form according to number, gender, and case.

3. In the singular number the article has the form an in all the cases except the genitive feminine, in which it becomes na; as caipleán na cipce, the castle of the hen.

In the plural number the article is always na.

4. In the spoken language the n of an is often omitted before a consonant; as ceann a ταιρb, the head of the bull. And this is sometimes found in books also, both printed and MS., but it is not to be recommended.

5. When an follows a preposition ending in a vowel, the a is often omitted in writing, but the omission is usually marked by an apostrophe; thus, ó an τíp, from the land, is written ó'n τíp; and pá an nɡpéin, under the sun, is written pa'n nɡpéin.

Very often in MSS., and sometimes in printed books, the apostrophe in such cases is omitted, and the n of the article joined with the preposition; as ón cíp, ɼán nɔpéin.

6. In the plural the article (na) is often joined to the preposition; as бona, for бo na.

7. The letter ɼ is inserted between certain prepositions and the article an; and this occasionally leads to combinations that might puzzle a learner. Thus ann an leabap, in the book, is written annɼ an leabap, and iɼ an leabap, which is still further shortened to ɼan leabap: also (omitting the n) annɼa leabap, and even ɼa leabap. And in the plural, iɼ na coppaib, "in the bodies."

II. CHANGES PRODUCED BY THE ARTICLE.

1. The article produces certain changes in the initial letters of nouns to which it is prefixed.

2. These changes are very important, and the learner will obtain a clearer view of them by separating the singular from the plural. For more on this subject, see page 31.

SINGULAR.

1. If the noun begins with an aspirable consonant (except ɼ, c, б), the article aspirates in the nominative feminine, and in the genitive masculine; as an bó, the cow; cuan an ɼiɼ ṁóiɼ, the harbour of the great man.

2. If the noun begins with ɼ, followed by a vowel or by l, n, or ɼ, the ɼ is eclipsed by c in those cases where, according to the last rule, a mutable consonant would be aspirated, as an c-ɼál (fem.), the heel; an c-ɼɼón (fem.), the nose; luaċ an c-ɼɼiain (masc.), the price of the bridle.

3. If the noun begins with a vowel, the article prefixes c to the nominative masculine, and h to the genitive feminine; as an c-aċaiɼ, the father; leabap na h-uiópe, the book of the dun (cow).

4. If the noun begins with an eclipsable consonant (except б or c), the article generally eclipses, if it be preceded by a simple preposition; as aiɼ

an g-cpann, on the tree; ó'n b-focal iber, "from the word 'iber;'" leir an b-fear, with the man.

5. But after the prepositions do and de, the article aspirates oftener than it eclipses; as ceitre céimc do'n érior, four degrees of the zone (Keating); do leanadar a g-cora do'n cappaig, their feet clung to the rock (story of the Children of Lir).

6. No change is produced by the article in the singular number, if the noun begins with l, n, r, d, t, or with f before a mute.

PLURAL.

1. If the noun begins with an eclipsable consonant, the article eclipses in the genitive; as inir na b-riobbad, [the] island of the woods; cailín dear crúióte na m-bó, [the] pretty girl of [the] milking of the cows (i.e., the pretty milking girl).

2. If the noun begins with a vowel, the article prefixes n to the genitive, and h to the other cases; as tír na n-óg, the land of the young (people); ó na h-áitib fin, from those places.

These are the only changes produced by the article in the plural.

CHAPTER II.

THE NOUN.

I. GENDER.

1. There are only two genders in the Irish language, the masculine and feminine: all Irish nouns, therefore, are either masculine or feminine gender.

2. In ancient Irish there was a neuter gender, but no trace of it remains in the modern language.

3. To know and remember the gender of all ordinary Irish nouns is one of the great difficulties in learning the language,

CHAP. II.]   THE NOUN.   19

as it is in learning French and many other languages. Without this knowledge, which can only be mastered by practice, no one can speak or write Irish correctly.

4. There are a few general rules which will very much help the learner to distinguish the gender of nouns: they are only *general* rules, however, subject to many exceptions; and where they do not apply, the student must depend on practice and memory.

MASCULINE.

1. The following nouns are generally masculine:—
(1.) Names of males; as coileac, a cock; laoc a hero; ꝼeaꞃ, a man.
(2.) Nouns of more than one syllable, ending in a consonant, or two consonants, preceded by a broad vowel; as boicceall, churlishness: except (*a*), derivatives in acc; (*b*), diminutives in óg.
(3.) Nouns ending in óiꞃ, aiꞃe, ac, aióe (or oióe, or uióe), when they denote personal agents, as they generally do; as ꞃpealaóóiꞃ, a mower; ꞃealgaiꞃe, a hunter; ceiceaꞃnac, a soldier—one of a body of *kerns;* ꞃgéalaióe or ꞃgéuluióe, a story-teller.
(4.) Diminutives in án and abstracts in aꞃ; as coileán, a whelp; cáiꞃdeaꞃ, friendship.
(5.) Diminutives in ín are of the same gender as the nouns from which they are derived.

FEMININE.

2. The following nouns are generally feminine:—
(1). Names of females; names of countries, rivers, and diseases; as ceaꞃc, a hen; Ciꞃe, Ireland; beaꞃba, the Barrow; pláig, a plague.
(2). Diminutives in óg, and derivatives in acc as ꝼuiꞃeóg, a lark; cuiꞃpacc, fragrance: and abstract nouns formed from the genitive feminine of adjectives; as baille, blindness.

(3). Nouns ending in a consonant, or in two consonants, preceded by a slender vowel (except those in óıp); as púıl, the eye ; póȝluım, learning

II. DECLENSIONS.

CASES.

1. Irish nouns have four cases, that is, four different inflections, to express relation :—Nominative, genitive, dative, and vocative.
2. The nominative case is the same as the nominative in English.
3. The genitive is the same as what is called the possessive case in English.
4. The dative is the case where a noun is governed by a preposition.
5. The vocative case is the same as what is called the nominative of address in English.
6. Irish nouns have different forms for these four cases, and for no others. Thus, the four cases of bpaḃán, a salmon, are for the plural number, as follows:—Nom. bpaḃáın, as τpí bpaḃáın, three salmons ; gen. bpaḃán, as loċ na m-bpaḃán, the lake of the salmons ; dat. bpaḃánaıḃ, as ḃo na bpaḃánaıḃ, to the salmons ; voc. bpaḃána, as a bpaḃána, ca ḃ-puıl pıḃ aȝ ḃul? "O ye salmons, whither are ye going?"
7. These four cases are not always different in form ; thus the four cases of the same noun in the singular number are:—Nom. bpaḃán ; gen. bpaḃáın ; dat. bpaḃán ; voc. bpaḃáın ; in which it will be seen that the dative is the same as the nominative, and the vocative the same as the genitive.
8. Those cases which are alike in form are distinguished by the sense ; just as the nominative and objective cases are distinguished in English.
9. Some writers on Irish grammar have put in two more cases, in imitation of Latin declension ; the accusative (or, as it is called in English, the objective) and the ablative. But in Irish there are no separate inflections for them, the accusative being always the same in form as the nominative.

CHAP. II.]   THE NOUN.   21

and the ablative the same as the dative; so that it would be only a useless puzzle to the learner to include them in a statement of Irish declension. In certain explanations, however, and in the statement of certain rules, it is sometimes convenient to speak of the accusative case.

10. Different nouns have different inflections for the same case; thus the datives singular of cop, a foot, and bop, a bush, are different, namely, coip and bop. But though this variation extends to most of the cases, the genitive singular is taken as the standard, in comparing the declension of one noun with the declension of another.

11. There are five chief ways of forming the genitive singular of Irish nouns; and in one or another of these ways, far the greatest number of nouns in the language form their genitive. There are usually reckoned, therefore, FIVE DECLENSIONS of Irish nouns.

12. Besides these there are other genitive inflections, but as no one of them comprises any considerable number of nouns, it is not considered necessary to lay down more than five declensions. The number of declensions is, however, very much a matter of convenience; and, accordingly, in some Irish grammars, there are more than five, and in some less.

FIRST DECLENSION.

1. The first declension comprises masculine nouns which have their characteristic vowel, that is, the last vowel of the nominative singular, broad.

2. The genitive singular is formed by attenuating the broad vowel.

3. In the singular, the dative is like the nominative, and the vocative is like the genitive; in the plural, the nominative is generally like the genitive singular, and the genitive like the nominative singular. Example, ball, a member or limb.

	Singular.		Plural.
Nom.*	baíll.	Nom.	baíll.
Gen.	baill.	Gen.	ball.
Dat.	ball.	Dat.	ballaıb.
Voc.	a baíll.	Voc.	a balla.

4. The number of nouns that belong to this declension is very large; but though they all form their genitive singular in the same way (except those in aċ, in which there is a slight additional change, for which see next paragraph), there are a few which vary in the formation of other cases.

5. Nouns in aċ, in addition to the attenuation, change ċ into ġ in the genitive singular; and generally form the nominative plural by adding e to the genitive singular; and from this again is formed the dative plural in ıb, in accordance with the rule in Par. 9, page 23. Example, marcaċ, a horseman.

	Singular.		Plural.
Nom.	marcaċ.	Nom.	marcaıġe.
Gen.	marcaıġ.	Gen.	marcaċ.
Dat.	marcaċ.	Dat.	marcaıġıb.
Voc.	a ṁarcaıġ.	Voc.	a ṁarcaċa.

6. A few nouns make their nominative plural by an increase in a; as peann, a pen; plur. peanna: and some of these are syncopated, as uball, an apple; plur. ubla.

7. In a few nouns of this declension the nominative plural is formed by adding ta or ċa to the nominative singular; as peól, a sail; nom. plur. peólta; dat. plur. peóltaıb: múr, a wall; nom. plur. múrċa; dat. plur. múrċaıb.

8. In many words of one syllable belonging to this declension, the attenuation in the genitive singular causes considerable change in the vowel or diphthongal part of the word; thus, corp, a body; gen. cuirp: iarġ, a fish; gen. éirġ:

---

* It would be well for the learner, when declining nouns, to call this "nominative and accusative" all through the declensions.

neapc, strength; gen. neipc or nipc: peap, a man; gen. pip: cpann, a tree; gen. cpoinn: béal, a mouth; gen. béil or beoil.

The three following rules (9, 10, and 11) apply to all the declensions.

9. The dative plural ends in ıb.

This ıb corresponds with the Latin dative and ablative termination *ibus* or *bus*. It is now very seldom pronounced, but it is nearly always retained in writing; just as in English, *gh*, which was formerly sounded as a guttural in such words as *plough, daughter*, is retained in writing, though it is no longer pronounced.

10. The dative plural is formed from the nominative plural whenever this latter differs from the genitive singular: otherwise from the nominative singular.

11. The vocative is always preceded by the particle a or O, which aspirates the initial; as a ṗip, O man; a ṁná, O women; O ťiǵeapna, O Lord.

SECOND DECLENSION.

1. The second declension comprises most of the feminine nouns in the language.

2. The genitive singular is formed by adding e to the nominative. If the characteristic vowel is broad, it must be attenuated in accordance with the rule caol le caol &c.

3. The dative singular is formed from the genitive singular by dropping the final e.

4. When the characteristic vowel is broad, the nominative plural is formed from the nominative singular by adding a; when the characteristic vowel is slender, by adding e.

5. The genitive plural is generally like the nominative singular.

6. The vocative is usually the same as the nominative, and is accordingly omitted from the paradigm.

First example, ꞃeɑmpóᵹ, a shamrock.

Singular.	Plural.
Nom. ꞃeɑmpóᵹ.	Nom. ꞃeɑmpóᵹɑ.
Gen. ꞃeɑmpóıᵹe.	Gen. ꞃeɑmpóᵹ.
Dat. ꞃeɑmpóıᵹ.	Dat. ꞃeɑmpóᵹɑıḃ.

Second example, péıꞃc, a worm, a beast.

Singular.	Plural.
Nom. péıꞃc.	Nom. péıꞃce.
Gen. péıꞃce.	Gen. péıꞃc.
Dat. péıꞃc.	Dat. péıꞃcıḃ.

7. Nouns in ɑċ, when they belong to this declension, change the ċ to ᵹ in the genitive singular: thus, cláıꞃꞃeɑċ, a harp, is declined as follows:—

Singular.	Plural.
Nom. cláıꞃꞃeɑċ.	Nom. cláıꞃꞃeɑċɑ.
Gen. cláıꞃꞃıᵹe.	Gen. cláıꞃꞃeɑċ.
Dat. cláıꞃꞃıᵹ.	Dat. cláıꞃꞃeɑċɑıḃ.

8. There are many nouns belonging to this declension which depart from the general rule laid down in Par. 4, in forming their nominative plural.

9. Some, probably over fifty, form the nominative plural by adding *ɑnnɑ;* and these form the genitive plural by dropping the final ɑ of this termination; thus, cúıꞃ, a cause; nom plural cúıꞃeɑnnɑ; gen. plural, cúıꞃeɑnn; dat. plural, cúıꞃeɑnnɑıḃ.

10. Some form their nominative plural by adding ɑċɑ: thus, oḃɑıꞃ, a work, and oꞃáıᴅ, a prayer, make oıḃꞃeɑċɑ and oꞃáıᴅeɑċɑ in the nominative plural.

11. When the characteristic vowel is slender, it is often dropped in the genitive plural; as ꝼuɑım, a sound; gen. plural ꝼuɑm.

12. When the nominative plural takes ce, the genitive plural is formed by adding ɑḋ; as coıll, a wood; nom. plur. coıllce; and genitive plural as

CHAP. II.] THE NOUN. 25

seen in Oileán na g-coillteaḋ, the island of the woods (Keating).

13. There are other variations of the nominative and genitive plural; but they do not comprise any considerable number of nouns, and they must be learned by practice.

THIRD DECLENSION.

1. Nouns belonging to the third declension are some of them masculine and some feminine.

2. The genitive singular is formed by adding a to the nominative singular.

3. The vocative is like the nominative.

4. The nominative plural is generally formed by adding a or e.

5. The genitive plural is generally like the nominative singular. Example, cleap, a trick or feat.

Singular.	Plural.
Nom. cleap.	Nom. cleapa.
Gen. cleapa.	Gen. cleap.
Dat. cleap.	Dat. cleapaiḃ.

6. If the characteristic vowel is slender, it must be made broad in the genitive singular, in accordance with the rule caol le caol &c.; as toil, the will, gen. tola.

7. Sometimes t or ṫ is introduced before the a of the genitive singular, which commonly causes other changes by syncope; as coḋail, sleep; gen. coḋalta: buaiḋirt, trouble, gen. buaiḋeartа.

8. This is the case with verbal or participial nouns in aḋ, eaḋ, and ugaḋ, the genitives of which have the same form as their passive participles considered as verbs; and they are all commonly reckoned as belonging to this declension, though the genitive singular is formed in some by adding

3

e, not a; as moladh, praising; gen, molta: ṗíneadh stretching; gen. ṗínte: caolughadh, making slender; gen. caoluighṫe.

9. Nouns in aċt generally, and those in ear or ior, often, belong to this declension; as cliṙteaċt, dexterity; gen. cliṙteaċta : doilġior, sorrow; gen. doilġiora. But the greater number of those in ear or ior belong to the first declension; thus the last noun, doilġior, is often made doilġir in the genitive; and bronntanar, a gift, makes bronntanair.

10. There are forty or fifty nouns (many of them ending in ir), which form their genitive singular in aċ, and which are reckoned as belonging to this declension, though some writers arrange them under a separate declension; as caṫair, a city; gen. caṫraċ : Teaṁair, Tara, gen. Teaṁraċ : ġráin, hatred; gen. ġránaċ.

11. Those in ir generally form their genitive as above; but aṫair, a father; máṫair, a mother; and bráṫair, a brother, form their genitive by dropping the final i:—gen. aṫar, máṫar, bráṫar.

12. Outside the general rule stated in Par. 4 above, there is considerable variety in the formation of the nominative plural.

13. Those in óir generally make the nominative plural by adding iḋe; as rpealadóir, a mower, nom. plur. rpealadóiriḋe.

14. And these form the genitive plural variously; generally na rpealadóiriḋ, but sometimes na rpealadóir or na rpealadórac.

15. Others form the nominative plural either like the genitive singular or by adding nna to it; as rruṫ, a stream; gen. rroṫa; nom. pl. rroṫa or rroṫanna : druim, a back; gen. droma; nom. plur. droma or dromanna.

16. Those that add nna, form the genitive plural by omitting the a; as ꞃpuċ; gen. plur. ꞃpuċann.

17. Many nouns of this declension that end in n or l, form their plural by adding ꞇe or ꞇa; as móin, a bog; gen. sing. móna; nom. plur. móinꞇe.

18. And these generally form their genitive plural by adding aḋ to the nominative plural; as móin; gen. plur. móinꞇeaḋ.

19. Those that form their genitive singular in aċ (10) form the plural by adding a to this aċ: as lapaip, a flame; gen. sing. lappaċ; nom. plur. lappaċa.

FOURTH DECLENSION.

1. Nouns of the fourth declension end in vowels or in ín, and are some of them masculine and some feminine.

2. There is no inflection in the singular, all the cases being alike.

3. The nominative plural is generally formed by adding íḋe or aḋa (with occasionally an obvious vowel change). Example, áipne, a sloe.

Singular.	Plural.
Nom. áipne.	Nom. áipníḋe.
Gen. áipne.	Gen. áipneaḋ.
Dat. áipne.	Dat. áipníḋiḃ.

4. Some form the plural by adding ꞇe or ċe: as ꞇeinne, a fire; nom. plur. ꞇeinnꞇe: ḃaoi, a clown; nom. plur. ḃaoiċe; and aiċne, a commandment, has nom. plur. aiċeanꞇa.

5. These generally form the genitive plural, by adding ḋ or aḋ (not to the nominative singular, as in the model, but) to the nominative plural: as nom. plur. ḃaoiċe, clowns; gen. plur. ḃaoiċeaḋ.

6. Nouns ending in aíḋe, uíḋe, and aipe, generally belong to this declension; as pclábuíḋe, a slave; píobaipe, a piper.

FIFTH DECLENSION.

1. Nouns of the fifth declension are mostly feminine.

2. They generally end in a vowel; and they form their genitive by adding n or nn, and occasionally ḋ or ṫ.

3. The dative singular is formed from the genitive by attenuation.

4. The nominative plural is formed from the genitive singular by adding a.

5. The genitive plural is like the genitive singular. Example, uppa, a door jamb.

Singular.	Plural.
Nom. uppa.	Nom. uppana.
Gen. uppan.	Gen. uppan.
Dat. uppain.	Dat. uppanaiḃ.

6. To this declension belong the proper names Eıre, Ireland; gen. Eıreann, dat. Eırınn: Alba, Scotland; gen., Alban, dat. Albaın: Muṁa, Munster; gen. Muṁan, dat. Muṁaın; and several others of less note.

7. Capa, a friend, is an example of the genitive in ḋ: nom. capa; gen. capaḋ; dat. capaıḋ; nom. plur. cáırḋe.

8. There is a good deal of variety in the formation of the cases of nouns belonging to this declension, which can only be learned by practice.*

IRREGULAR DECLENSION.

1. Some nouns are irregular; that is, they are not inflected in accordance with any of the regular declensions.

2. The most important of the irregular nouns are:*—bean, a woman; bó, a cow; bpú, a womb;

---

*For additional examples of declensions of nouns, both regular and irregular, see Appendix at the end of the book.

CHAP. II.]   THE NOUN.   29

caoṗa, a sheep; ceó, a fog; cnó, a hut; cú, a hound; Ḋia, God; lá, a day; mí, a month; o or ua, a grandson. They are declined as follows. (The vocative is not given where it is like the nominative.)

bean, *a woman, fem.*

Singular	Plural
Nom. bean.	Nom mná
Gen. mná.	Gen. ban
Dat. mnaoi.	Dat. mnáib.

bó, *a cow, fem.*

Nom. bó.	Nom. bá
Gen. bó.	Gen. bó
Dat. buin.	Dat. búaib.

bṗú, *a womb, fem.*

Nom. bṗú	Nom bṗonna.
Gen. bṗuinne or bṗonn.	Gen. bṗonn
Dat. bṗoinn.	Dat bṗonnaiḃ

Caoṗa, *a sheep, fem.*

Nom. caoṗa.	Nom. caoiṗiġ,
Gen. caoṗać.	Gen. caoṗać.
Dat. caoṗa.	Dat. caoṗċaib.
Voc. a ċaoṗa	Voc. a ċaoṗċa.

Ceó, *a fog, masc.*

Nom. ceó.	Nom. ciaḋ.
Gen. ciaċ or ceoiṡ.	Gen. ceó.
Dat. ceó.	Dat. ceóċaiḃ.

Cnó or cnú, *a nut, masc.*

Nom. cnó.	Nom. cná, cnai.
Gen. cnó, cnui.	Gen. cnóḃ
Dat. cnó, cnú.	Dat. cnáiḃ.

3*

30   ETYMOLOGY.   [PART II.

Cú, *a hound, masc. or fem.*

Nom. cú.   Nom. coin, cuin, cona, or cointe.
Gen. con.   Gen. con.
Dat. coin.   Dat. conaib.

Dia, *God, masc.*

Nom. Dia.   Nom. Dée, Déitc.
Gen. Dé.   Gen. Dia, Déiteaḋ.
Dat. Dia.   Dat. Déib Déitib.
Voc. a Ḋhé or a Ḋhia.   Voc. a Ḋhée, Ḋhéitc.

Lá, *a day, masc.*

Nom. lá.   Nom. laete.
Gen. lae.   Gen. laeteaḋ, lá.
Dat. lá, ló.   Dat. laetib.

Mí, *a month, fem.*

Nom. mí.   Nom. míora.
Gen. míṗ, míora.   Gen. míoṗ.
Dat. mí, míṗ.   Dat. míoraib.

O or ua, *a grandson, masc.*

Nom. ó, ua.   Nom. uí.
Gen. i, uí.   Gen. ua.
Dat. o, ua.   Dat. ib, uib.
Voc. a, uí.   Voc. a, uí.

DECLENSION OF THE ARTICLE WITH THE NOUN.

1. The initial changes produced by the article in the nouns to which it is prefixed have been set forth at page 17; these changes must be carefully observed in declining nouns with the article.

CHAP. II.]   THE NOUN.   31

2. Twelve typical examples are here given, corresponding with the several cases mentioned in paragraphs 1, 2, 3, 4, 5, and 6, pages 17, 18; and these examples include almost every possible variety. There is a good deal of difference of usage in the dative singular of nouns beginning with ſ.

3. The declension of the singular number only is given; the changes in the plural are so very simple (see page 18) that they can present no difficulty.

4. Colᵹ, a sword, masc. Nom. an colᵹ; gen. an cuilᵹ; dat. leiſ an ᵹ-colᵹ (Par. 4, p. 17), or do'n ċolᵹ (Par. 5, p. 18).

5. Cailleaċ, a hag, fem. Nom. an ċailleaċ; na cailliᵹe; dat. ó'n ᵹ-cailliᵹ or do'n ċailliᵹ.

6. Saoᵹal, the world, masc. Nom. an ſaoᵹal; gen. an c-ſaoᵹail; dat. ó'n ſaoᵹal or do'n c-ſaoᵹal (Par 5, p. 18).

7. Sabóid, the Sabbath, fem. Nom an c-Sabóid; gen. na Sabóide; dat. ó'n Sabóid or do'n c-Sabóid (Pars. 2 and 5, pp. 17 and 18.)

8. Slac, a rod, fem. Nom. an c-ſlac; gen. na ſlaice; dat. leiſ an ſlaic or do'n c-ſlaic.

9. Sſól, satin, masc. Nom. an ſſól; gen. an c-ſſóil; dat. ó'n ſſól or do'n c-ſſól.

10. Aſal, an ass, masc. Nom. an c-aſal; gen. an aſail; dat. ó'n aſal.

11. Iniſ, an island, fem. Nom. an iniſ; gen. na h-inſe; dat. do'n iniſ.

12. Leac, a stone, fem. Nom. an leac; gen. na leice; dat. do'n leic (Par. 6, p. 18).

13. Díle, a deluge, fem. Nom. an díle; gen na díleann; dat. do'n dílinn

14. Sᵹeul, a story, masc. Nom. an ſᵹeul; gen an ſᵹéil; dat. ó'n ſᵹeul.

15. Speal, a scythe, fem. Nom. an ſpeal; gen. na ſpeile; dat. leiſ an ſpeil.

CHAPTER III.

THE ADJECTIVE.

I. DECLENSION OF ADJECTIVES.

1. In Irish the adjective changes its form according to the gender, case, and number of the noun.

2. Adjectives are declined in much the same manner as nouns; but they never take the inflection ıḃ in the dative plural (though anciently they had this inflection like nouns): the dative plural of an adjective is like the nominative plural.

3. There are usually reckoned four declensions of adjectives.

4. The inflections of these four declensions follow those of the noun so closely, that when the noun is mastered the adjective presents no difficulty.

FIRST DECLENSION.

1. Adjectives of the first declension are those that end in a consonant preceded by a broad vowel, as bán, white; pluċ, wet.

2. In the masculine gender (i.e., when the adjective belongs to a masculine noun), they are declined the same as nouns of the first declension of the type of ball, except that the nominative plural always ends in a.

3. In the feminine gender adjectives are declined the same as nouns of the second declension of the type of ꞃeampóg.

4. Both genders are alike in the plural. Example, bán, white.

CHAP. III.] THE ADJECTIVE. 33

	Singular.		Plural.	
	Masc.	Fem.	Masc. and Fem.	
Nom.	bán.	bán.	Nom.	bána.
Gen.	báin.	báine.	Gen.	bán.
Dat.	bán.	báin.	Dat.	bána.
Voc.	báin.	bán.	Voc.	bána.

SECOND DECLENSION.

1. Adjectives of the second declension are those that end in a consonant preceded by a slender vowel.
2. In the singular, all the cases of both masculine and feminine are alike, except the genitive feminine, which takes e.
3. In the plural, both genders are alike, and all the cases except the genitive are formed by adding e; the genitive is like the nominative singular. Example, mín, smooth, fine.

	Singular.		Plural.	
	Masc.	Fem.	Masc. and Fem.	
Nom.	mín.	mín.	Nom.	míne.
Gen.	mín.	míne.	Gen.	mín.
Dat.	mín.	mín	Dat.	míne.
Voc.	mín.	mín.	Voc.	míne.

THIRD DECLENSION.

1. Adjectives of the third declension are those that end in amail, which has the same signification as the English postfix *like* :—bean, a woman banamail, womanlike, modest.
2. The two genders are always alike.
3. The four cases singular are alike except the genitive, which is formed by adding a, with a syncope.
4. In the plural, the genitive is the same as the nominative singular; and the other cases are the same as the genitive singular. Example, maipeamail, graceful.

Singular.	Plural.
Nom. maɪrcaṁaɪl.	Nom. maɪreaṁla.
Gen. maɪreaṁla.	Gen. maɪreaṁaɪl.
Dat. maɪreaṁaɪl.	Dat. maɪreaṁla.

FOURTH DECLENSION.

1. Adjectives of the fourth declension are those that end in vowels; as mópòa, majestic.

2. They have no inflections, being alike in all cases, numbers, and genders.

II. DECLENSION OF THE ADJECTIVE AND ARTICLE WITH THE NOUN.

1. The rules for the aspiration of the initial consonants of adjectives agreeing with nouns are given at p. 10; and these rules must be very carefully observed in declining nouns with adjectives.

2. It may be added here that ḃ and c sometimes resist aspiration, especially if they follow a noun ending in n. There is much variety of usage as to aspiration of adjectives in the dative singular.

3. When a noun is declined with both an adjective and the article, the initial of the adjective is generally eclipsed in the genitive plural (or takes n if it be a vowel).

4. Four typical examples are here given of the declension of the adjective with the noun. For the influence of the article see p. 17.

An capall bán, *the white horse, masc.*

Singular.	Plural.
Nom. an capall bán.	na capaıll bána.
Gen. an ċapaıll ḃáın.	na ɜ-capall m-bán.
Dat. ó'n ɜ-capall ḃán or m-bán.	ó'na capallaıḃ bána.
Voc. a ċapaıll ḃáın.	a ċapalla bána.

THE ADJECTIVE.

An ṗuireóġ beaġ, *the little lark, fem.*

Nom. an ṗuireóġ beaġ.
Gen. na ṗuiréoiġe biġe.
Dat. ó'n ḃ-ṗuiṙeoiġ ḃiġ.
Voc. a ṗuiṙeóġ ḃeaġ.

Nom. na ṗuiṙeóġa beaġa.
Gen. na ḃ-ṗuiṙeóġ m-ḃeaġ.
Dat. ó'na ṗuiṙeóġaiḃ beaġa.
Voc. a ṗuiṙeóġa beaġa.

An cnoc árd, *the high hill, masc.*

Nom. an cnoc árd.
Gen. an ċnuic áird.
Dat. o'n ġ-cnoc árd.
Voc. a ċnuic áird.

Nom. na cnuic árda.
Gen. na ġ-cnoc n-árd.
Dat. ó'na cnocaiḃ árda.
Voc. a ċnoca árda.

An bó duḃ, *the black cow, fem.*

Nom. an bó duḃ.
Gen. na bó duiḃe.
Dat. do'n m-buin duiḃ.
Voc. a bó duḃ.

Nom. na ba duḃa.
Gen. na m-bó n-duḃ.
Dat. do na búaiḃ duḃa.
Voc. a ḃa duḃa.

III. COMPARISON OF ADJECTIVES.

1. Irish adjectives have three degrees of comparison, the same as English adjectives.

2. The positive is the simple form of the adjective; as árd, high; plaiċeaṁail, princely.

3. The comparative and the superlative have the same form, which is that of the genitive singular feminine; as áirde, plaiċeaṁla; and they are distinguished by prefixed particles, or by the context.

4. The comparative has generally the particle níor (or níora or níra) prefixed, and it is usually followed by ná, than (spelled also iná and ioná); as tá an teaċ ro níor áirde ná an teaċ ṙin, this house is higher than that house: atá an laoċ úd níop plaiċeaṁla ná an píġ péin, "yonder champion is more princely than the king himself."

5. The superlative is often preceded by ip or ap, with the article expressed before the noun; as an peap ip plaiċeaṁla pan típ, the most princely man in the country.

6. In the comparative, níop is omitted when the assertion or question is made by the verb ip in any of its forms, expressed or understood; as ba ouibe a ġpuaġ ná an ġual, "her hair was blacker than the coal;" ip ġile pneaċta ná bainne, snow is whiter than milk; an peápp do ḋeapbpaċaip ná ċúpa? is thy brother better than thou?

7. When the characteristic particles are not expressed, the construction generally determines whether the adjective is comparative or superlative; as an ealaḋan ip uaiple ná piliḋeaċt, the art which is nobler than poetry; an ealaḋan ip uaiple aip biċ, "the art which is the noblest in the world."

8. An adjective in the comparative or superlative is not inflected; all the cases being alike in form.

IRREGULAR COMPARISON.

1. The following adjectives are irregularly compared. There are a few others, but their departure from rule is so slight as not to require notice.

2. Lia is a comparative as it stands, signifying more (in number); but it has no positive, unless iomḋa or mópán (many), or some such word, be considered as such.

CHAP. III.]   THE ADJECTIVE.   37

Positive.	Comparative.	Superlative.
beaʒ, little.	níor luɣa.	ır luɣa.
pada, long.	níor paıde, níor ría.	ır paıde, ır ría.
pupur or upur, easy.	níor pura, níor ura.	ır pura, ır ura.
maıt, deaɣ, } good.	níor peárr.	ır peárr.
mınıc, often.	níor mıonca.	
mór, great.	níor mó.	ır mó.
olc, bad.	níor meara.	ır meara.
teıt, hot.	níor teó.	ır teó.

3. There are certain particles which, when prefixed to adjectives, intensify their signification; and in accordance with the rule in Par. 4, page 10, they aspirate the initials of the adjectives.

4. The principal of these are an, píor, pó, rár, úr : as maıt, good ; an-ṁaıt, very good : ʒránna, ugly ; píor-ʒránna, excessively ugly : mór, large ; pó-ṁór, very large : láıdır, strong ; rár-láıdır, very strong, &c.

IV. NUMERAL ADJECTIVES.

1. The following is a list of the most important of the numerals, both cardinal and ordinal.

For the influence of some of them in aspirating and eclipsing, and for other syntactical influences on the noun, see Syntax.

Cardinal.		Ordinal.	
1.	aon.	1st.	céad.
2.	dó, dá.	2nd.	dara.
3.	trí, treóra.	3rd.	trear.
4.	ceataır, ceıtre.	4th.	ceatraṁad.
5.	cúıʒ.	5th.	cúıʒead.
6.	ré.	6th.	reıread.
7.	reatt.	7th.	reattṁad.
8.	ott.	8th.	ottṁad.
9.	naoı.	9th.	naoṁad.
10.	deıc.	10th.	deacṁad.
11.	aon déaʒ.	11th.	aonṁad déaʒ.

4

38 ETYMOLOGY. [PART II

12.	dó déag, dá déag.	12th.	dara déag.
13.	trí déag.	13th.	treap déag.
	And so on, up to and including 19.		
20.	fice.	20th.	ficead.
21.	aon a'r fice, aon air ficid, And so on, up to 29.	21st.	aonṁad air ficid.
30.	trioċad, trioċa, deiċ a'r fice.	30th.	trioċadad, deaċṁad air ficid.
33.	trí air trioċaid, trí déag a'r fice.	33rd.	treap air trioċaid, treap déag air ficid.
40.	dá ficid, ceaṫraċa, ceaṫraċad.	40th.	ceaṫraċadad.
50.	caoga, caogad.	50th.	caogadad.
60.	reargad, rearga, trí ficid.	60th.	reargadad, trí ficidead.
70.	reaċtṁoga, reaċtṁogad, deiċ a'r trí ficid.	70th.	reaċtṁogadad, deaċṁad air trí ficid.
80.	oċtṁoga, oċtṁogad, ceitre ficid.	80th.	oċtmogadad, ceitre ficidead.
90.	noċa, noċad, deiċ a'r ceitre ficid	90th.	noċadad, deaċṁad air ceitre ficid.
100.	céad.	100th.	céadad.
1,000.	míle.	1,000th.	mílead.
2,000.	dá ṁíle.	2,000th.	dá ṁílead.
1,000,000.	milliún.	1,000,000th.	milliúnad.

2. Dó and ceaṫair are used only in the absence of nouns, i.e. merely as the names of the numbers; but dá and ceitre are always used when the nouns are expressed; as dá ċluair, two ears; ceitre fir, four men.

3. Fice is declined :—Nom. fice; gen. ficead; dat. ficid; nom. plur. ficid.

4. Céad has gen. céid; nom. pl. céada or céadta.

5. The following nouns, which are all except

beiɼc, formed from the numerals, are applied to persons only:—

ḃfaɼ,ḃíɼ, two persons.	ɼeaȯċaɼ,	} seven persons.
beiɼc, a couple.	móɼ-ɼeiɼeaɼ,	
cɼiúɼ, three persons.	oċċaɼ,	eight ,,
ceaċɼaɼ, four ,,	nonḃaɼ, naonḃaɼ,	nine ,,
cúiʒeaɼ, five ,,	ḃeiċneaḃaɼ,	ten ,,
ɼeiɼeaɼ, six ,,		

CHAPTER IV.

THE PRONOUN.

1. There are in Irish six kinds of pronouns:— Personal, Possessive, Relative, Demonstrative, Interrogative, and Indefinite.

I. PERSONAL PRONOUNS.

1. There are four personal pronouns—mé, I, tú, thou; ɼé, he; ɼí, she; with their plurals, ɼinn, we; ɼiḃ, ye or you; and ɼiaḋ, they. These are the simple forms of the personal pronouns.

2. Each of these takes an emphatic increase or postfixed syllable, equivalent to the English word *self;* and the whole word thus formed is called the emphatic form. The emphatic syllables vary their vowel part in accordance with the rule caol le caol &c.

3. The following are the emphatic forms:— Miɼe or meɼi, myself; túɼa, thyself; ɼéɼean, himself; sise, herself; sinne, ourselves; siḃse, yourselves; siadsan, themselves.

4. The word féin, self, is often added to the personal pronouns, not as a particle but as a separate word; and it is still more emphatic than the particles mentioned in last paragraph:—mé féin, I myself; sí féin, she herself.

5. The personal pronouns are all declined; and they may carry the emphatic increase through all the cases.

6. The personal pronouns (except mé), unlike nouns, have a distinct form for the accusative (or objective) case. It is, of course, only the pronoun tú that is used in the vocative.

DECLENSION OF PERSONAL PRONOUNS.

The declension of the emphatic form of mé is given as an example: observe, in this, the vowel changes in obedience to caol le caol &c.

Mé, *I*.

Singular.	Plural.
Nom. mé, I.	Nom. sinn, we.
Gen. mo, mine.	Gen. ár, our.
Dat. dom, daṁ, to me.	Dat. dúinn, to us.
Acc. mé, me.	Acc. inn or sinn, us.

Mise, *myself* (*emphatic form*).

Nom. mise, mesi, myself.	Nom. sinne, ourselves.
Gen. mo-sa, my own.	Gen. ár-ne, our own.
Dat. domsa, daṁsa, to myself.	Dat. dúinne, to ourselves
Acc. mise, mesi, myself.	Acc. inne, sinne, ourselves.

Tú, *thou*.

Nom. tú.	Nom. siḃ.
Gen. do.	Gen. ḃur, ḃar.
Dat. duit.	Dat. daoiḃ, díḃ.
Acc. ṫú.	Acc. iḃ, siḃ.
Voc. ṫú.	Voc. siḃ, iḃ.

Sé, *he.*

Nom. sé.
Gen a.
Dat. do
Acc. é.

Nom. siad.
Gen. a.
Dat. dóib
Acc. iad.

Sí, *she.*

Nom. sí
Gen a
Dat. di
Acc. í

Nom siad.
Gen. a
Dat. dóib.
Acc iad.

PERSONAL PRONOUNS COMPOUNDED WITH PREPOSITIONS.

1 In Irish, the personal and the possessive pronouns unite with prepositions, each compound forming a single word.

2 In each case the preposition and the pronoun are amalgamated, and the latter changes its form, so as to be considerably, and in some cases completely, disguised.

3. These "prepositional pronouns," as they are sometimes called, are of constant occurrence in the language—scarce a sentence in which they are not met with : they are therefore of great importance, and the learner should get them all off by heart

4. The following prepositions unite with personal pronouns.—ag; air or ar; ann or i; ar; cum, de; do; eidir or idir, fá or faoi; le; o or ua; roim, reac, tar; tré; uar; um or im.

5. The following are the combinations of these prepositions with the personal pronouns

6. The emphatic particles may be used with these combinations also, as well as with the uncompounded pronouns, of which one example is given.

Ag, at or with.

Singular.
agam, with or at me.
agat, agad, with thee.
aige, with him.
aice or aici, with her.

Plural.
againn, with us.
agaib, with you.
aca or acu, with them.

The same with the emphatic increase.

agamra, with myself.
agatra, with thyself.
aigerean, with himself.
aicire, with herself.

againne, with ourselves.
agaibre, with yourselves.
acaran, with themselves.

Air or ar, upon.

orm, on me.
ort, on thee.
air, on him.
uirre, on her.

orrainn, on us.
orraib, on you.
orra, orta, on them.

Ann or i, in.

ionnam, in me.
ionnat, ionnad, in thee.
ann, in him.
innte, innti, in her.

ionnainn, ionainn, in us.
ionnaib, in you.
ionnta, in them.

As, out of.

asam, out of me.
asat, asad, out of thee.
as, out of him.
aiste, aisti, out of her.

asainn, out of us.
asaib, out of you.
asta, astu, out of them.

Cum, towards, unto.

cugam, unto me.
cugat, unto thee.
cuige, unto him.
cuici, unto her.

cugainn, unto us.
cugaib, unto you.
cuca, unto them.

De, from or off.

diom, off or of me.
diot, off thee.
de, off him.
di, off her.

dinn, off us.
dib, off you.
diob, off them.

CHAP. IV.]   THE PRONOUN.   43

Do, *to.*

dam, dom, daṁ, to me.   dúinn, to us.
duit, to thee.   daoib, díb, to you.
do, to him.   dóib, to them.
di, to her.

Eidir, *between.*

eadram, between me.   eadrainn, between us.
eadrat, between thee.   eadraib, between you.
eidir é, between him.   eatorra, between them.
eidir í, between her.

Fá or Faoi, *under.*

fúm, under me.   fúinn, under us.
fút, under thee,   fúib, under you.
faoi, under him.   fúta, under them.
fúiṫe, under her.

Le, *with.*

liom, with me.   linn, with us.
leat, with thee.   lib, with you.
leip, with him.   leó, with them.
léiṫe, léi, with her.

Le is often written re in books, and its pronominal combinations in this form are often met with. They are as follows:—

riom, with me.   rinn, with us.
riot, with thee.   rib, with you.
rir, with him.   riu, with them.
ria, with her.

O or ua, *from.*

uaim, from me.   uainn, from us.
uait, from thee.   uaib, from you.
uað, from him.   uata, from them.
uaiṫe, uaiṫi, from her.

Roiṁ, *before.*

róṁam, before me.   róṁainn, before us.
róṁat, before thee.   róṁaib, before you.
róiṁe, before him.   rómpa, before them.
róimpe, róimpi, before her.

Seaċ, *beside.*

ɼeaċam, beside me.
ɼeaċaṫ, beside thee.
ɼeaċ é, beside him.
ɼeaċ í, beside her.

ɼeaċainn, beside us.
ɼeaċaiḃ, beside you.
ɼeaċa, beside them.

Tar, *beyond, over.*

ṫorm, ṫarm, over me.
ṫorṫ, ṫarṫ, over thee.
ṫairir, over him.
ṫairrṫe, ṫairri, over her.

ṫorrainn, ṫarrainn, over us.
ṫorraiḃ, ṫarraiḃ, over you.
ṫarrṫa, ṫarra, over them.

Tre, *through.*

triom, through me.
trioṫ, through thee.
triḋ, through him.
triċe, triċi, through her.

trinn, through us.
triḃ, through you.
trioṫa, through them.

Uar, *above.*

uaram, above me.
uaraṫ, above thee.
uara, above him.
uairṫe, uairṫi, above her.

uarainn, above us.
uaraiḃ, above you.
uarṫa, above them.

Um or im, *about.*

umam, about me.
umaṫ, about thee.
uime, about him.
uimpe, uimpi, about her.

umainn, about us.
umaiḃ, about you.
umpa, about them.

II. POSSESSIVE PRONOUNS.

1. The possessive pronouns, which are merely the genitives of the personal pronouns, are as follows:—mo, my; ḋo, thy; a, his or her; ár, our; ḃar or ḃur, your; a, their. The three possessives, a, his, a, her, and a, their, are distinguished by the initial letter changes of the next word. (See pp. 9, 11, 12; and see also Syntax.)

2. The o of mo and do is omitted before a vowel or before ṗ; as m'aċaıɼ, my father; m'ṗeaɼann, my land. And do is often changed, before a vowel, to c, ċ, and h; as c'aċaıɼ, ċ'aċaıɼ, or h-aċaıɼ, thy father.

3. The possessive pronouns also take the emphatic increase, with this peculiarity, however, that the emphatic particle always follows the noun that comes after the possessive, or if the noun be qualified by one or more adjectives, the emphatic particle comes last of all; and in accordance with the rule caol le caol, its vowel is generally broad or slender according as the last vowel of the word it follows is broad or slender; as mo ċeaċ-ɼa, my house, or my own house; mo ċeaċ móɼ buıde-ɼı, my great yellow house. And these again may be followed by ɼéın (Par. 4, p. 40), rendering the expression still more emphatic; as mo ċeaċ-ɼa ɼéın, my own house.

POSSESSIVE PRONOUNS COMPOUNDED WITH PREPOSITIONS.

1. The possessive pronouns are amalgamated with prepositions, much in the same way as the personal pronouns; as beıɼ beannaċċ óm ċɼoıde, bear a blessing *from my* heart.

2. The following are the most important of these combinations:—

ann, *in.*

Singular.	Plural.
am, am', in my.	ınáɼ, 'náɼ, in our.
ad, ad', in thy.	—
ıona, ına, 'na, in his or her.	ıona, ına, 'na, in their.

do, *to.*

dom, dom', to my.	dáɼ, d'áɼ, to our.
dod, dod', to thy.	—
dá, da, to his or her.	dá, d'a, to their.

Le, *with.*

lem, lem', with my.   lep, le'p, with our
leb, leb', with thy.   —
lena, le n-a, with his or her.   lena, le n-a, with their,

O or ua *from.*

óm, óm', from my.   oáp, ó'p, from our.
ób, ób', from thy.   —
óna, ó n-a, from his or her.   óna, o n-a, from their.

3. Those that are identical in form and different in meaning are distinguished by the initial letter changes they produce in the next word; as óna ċıġ, from his house; óna cıġ, from her house; óna b-cıġ, from their house.

4. These combinations can also take the emphatic increase, like those of the personal pronouns, with the peculiarity, however, noticed in Par. 3, p. 45; as óm ċıġ móp ápb-pa, from my great high house.

III. RELATIVE PRONOUNS.

1. There are three relative pronouns in Irish:— a, who, which, that; noċ, who, which, that; naċ, which not; as an cé a buaıleap, the person who strikes; an lıaıġ noċ a beıp ġo b-puıl cú plán, the physician that says that you are well; an cé naċ b-puıl láıbıp, ní puláıp bó beıċ ġlıc, "the person who is not strong, it is necessary for him to be wise."

2. Dá sometimes takes the place of the relative a; and in some grammars it is counted as a distinct relative pronoun; as cáıb na ġaolca ıp peápp aġum bá b-puıl a b-calaıṁ Epeann, "I have

CHAP. IV.] THE PRONOUN. 47

the best friends *that are* (to be found) in the land of Erin." And sometimes ʋo stands for the relative a.

3. The relative a has sometimes the sense of "all which" or "all that;" as beip beannaċṫ ċum a maipeannʋe piolpaiċ Ip a'p Eiƀip, "bear a blessing to *all that* live of the seed of Ir and Eber;" a ƀ-puil pan ċalaṁ ʋ'aicme Mháine, "*all that* are in the land of the tribe of Máinè."

4. The relative pronouns are not declined.

IV. DEMONSTRATIVE PRONOUNS.

1. The demonstrative pronouns are po, this, these; pin, that, those; púʋ or úʋ, yonder: as an peap po, this man; na mná pin, those women; púʋ í píop, "yonder she (moves) below."

V. INTERROGATIVE PRONOUNS.

1. There are usually reckoned three interrogative pronouns:—cia or cé, who? cá, what? where? caʋ or cpeuʋ, what? as cia ċpúṫuiġ ṫú? who created thee? caʋ ʋeip ṫú? what sayest thou? ca ƀ-puil an peap pin? where is that man? cpeuʋ ip éiġin? what is necessary?

VI. INDEFINITE PRONOUNS.

1. The following are the principal indefinite pronouns:—

aon, one.
éiġin, some, certain.
eile, aile, other.
cáċ, all.
ġaċ, each, every.
ġaċ uile, every.

ceaċtap, either.
uile, all.
a céile, each other.
an té, an tí, the person who.
cia b'é, cibé, ġibé, whoever.

2. The indefinite pronouns are not declined; except cáċ, which has a genitive form, cáıċ; and ꒳aċ, which is sometimes made ꒳aċa in the genitive.

CHAPTER V.

THE VERB.

1. Irish verbs are inflected for number, person, mood, tense, and voice.

2. The conjugation is arranged, not according to the initial changes, but according to terminations.

3. As to the initial changes:—see pages 10 and 58 for the particles that aspirate, and page 12 for the particles that eclipse, the initials of verbs.

I. PERSONS: SYNTHETIC AND ANALYTIC FORMS.

1. The verb has three persons singular and three persons plural; and it has inflections for the whole six in the indicative and conditional moods of the active voice, except in one tense of the indicative.

2. The six forms of the present tense, indicative mood, active voice, of the verb tó꒳, take, are as follows:—

Singular.	Plural.
1. tó꒳aım, I take.	1. tó꒳amaoıḋ, we take.
2. tó꒳aıp, thou takest.	2. tó꒳ċaoı, ye take.
3. tó꒳aıḋ ré, he takes.	3. tó꒳aıḋ, they take.

CHAP. V.] THE VERB. 49

3. This is what is called the synthetic form of the verb. The synthetic form is that in which the persons are expressed by inflections or terminations.

4. These six forms express the sense perfectly, without the accompaniment of the pronouns (except in the case of the third person singular): that is, τόɣαιρ, as it stands, without using along with it the pronoun τú, thou, expresses perfectly "thou takest;" and so of the others.

5. But there is another way of expressing the persons, singular and plural, namely, by using one form of the verb for the whole six, and putting in the pronouns to distinguish the persons and numbers. This is what is called the analytic form of the verb.

6. In this analytic mode of expressing the persons and numbers, the form of the verb that is used is the same as the form for the third person singular; and the persons singular and plural are expressed as follows:—

Singular.   Plural.
1. τόɣαιὂ mé, I take.   1. τόɣαιὂ ριnn, we take.
2. τόɣαιὂ τú, thou takest.   2. τόɣαιὂ ριὂ, ye take.
3. τόɣαιὂ ρé, he takes.   3. τόɣαιὂ ριαὂ, they take.

7. The third singular of the verb is not a synthetic form like the other five, that is, it does not include the pronoun as they do. In the third person singular, therefore, the pronoun must be always expressed in order to distinguish the number and person; unless there is a noun, or that the nominative is in some other way obvious from the construction.

8. But generally speaking it is not allowable to express any other pronoun along with the corresponding synthetic form of the verb:—For example, it would be wrong to say ᵭéanaim mé or ᵭéanamaoiᵭ pinn, both expressions being tautological.

9. This rule, in the case of the third person plural, however, is sometimes not observed; for such expressions as molaiᵭ piaᵭ and molpaiᵭ piaᵭ—they praise, they will praise—are often met with, though molaiᵭ or molpaiᵭ alone would answer. And a like construction (in the third plural) is often used when the nominative is a plural noun, both in the present and in the past tense; as cpiallaiᵭ mic Mileaᵭ, "the sons of Milè go;" map ᵭo concaᵭap na ᵭpaoiċe, "when the druids saw."

10. The emphatic particles may be postfixed to all the persons of verbs, in the same manner as to pronouns and nouns (p. 39); as molaim-pe, I praise; molaip-pe, thou praisest. And in all such cases, the word péin (p. 40) may be used to make the expression still more emphatic; as ᵭo ċuippinn-pe péin mo leanᵭ a ċoᵭlaᵭ, "I myself would put my child to sleep."

11. The general tendency of modern languages is to drop synthetic forms, and to become more analytic. The English language, for example, has lost nearly all its inflections, and supplied their place by prepositions, conjunctions, adverbs, and auxiliary verbs. Following this tendency, the synthetic forms of the Irish verb are falling into disuse in the spoken language; and it has been already remarked (p. 23) that the noun-inflection iᵭ is now seldom used in speaking. But all these forms are quite common in even the most modern Irish books; and the learner must, therefore, make himself quite familiar with them.

II. TENSES.

1. In English a regular verb has only two different forms to express tense:—I love, I loved;

CHAP. V.] THE VERB. 51

all the other tenses are expressed by means of auxiliaries.

2. In Irish, a regular verb has five different forms in the indicative mood for tense. Reckoning those tenses only which are expressed by inflection, an Irish regular verb has therefore FIVE TENSES in the indicative mood.

3. The five tenses with the synthetic forms for the first person singular of the regular verb ᵹoıp, call, are:—

(1.) The present; ᵹoıpım, I call.

(2.) The consuetudinal or habitual present; ᵹoıpeann mé, I am in the habit of calling.

(3.) The past, or simple past, or perfect (for it is known by all these three names); ꝺo ᵹoıpeap, I called.

(4.) The consuetudinal or habitual past; ꝺo ᵹoıpınn, I used to call, or I used to be calling.

(5.) The future; ᵹoıppeaꝺ, I shall or will call.

III. MOODS AND VOICES.

1. The Irish regular verb has four moods:— The Imperative, the Indicative, the Conditional, and the Infinitive. These are the only moods for which the regular verb has distinct inflections.

2. There are, indeed, other moods, which are expressed, not by inflection, but by means of certain conjunctions and particles set before the verb; and these additional moods are given in conjugation in some Irish grammars; but as their forms do not differ from the forms of the four given in the last paragraph, they are not included here.

3. It is only the indicative mood of the verb that has tense inflection; in each of the other moods there is only one tense.

4. There are two voices, the active and the passive. It is only in the active voice that there are personal inflections; in the passive voice, the three persons singular and the three persons plural have all six the same form, rendering it necessary, of course, that the pronoun be always expressed when there is no noun.

IV. CONJUGATION OF A REGULAR VERB.

buail, *strike*.

ACTIVE VOICE

IMPERATIVE MOOD.

Singular.	Plural.
1.	1. buailimír, let us strike.
2. buail, strike thou.	2. buailíð, strike ye.
3. buaileað ré, let him strike.	3. buailíoír, let them strike.

INDICATIVE MOOD.

Present Tense.

Singular.	Plural.
1. buailim, I strike.	1. buailimíð, we strike.
2. buailir, thou strikest.	2. buailtí, ye strike.
3. buailíð ré, he strikes.	3. buailíð, they strike.

(*For the relative form of this tense, see p.* 55.)

Consuetudinal or habitual Present.

buaileann mé, *I usually strike.*
(*The same form for all persons and numbers.*)

CHAP. V.] THE VERB. 53

Past.

1. buaileap, I struck.
2. buailip, thou struckest.
3. buail ré, he struck.

1. buaileamap, we struck.
2. buaileabap, ye struck.
3. buaileabap, they struck.

Old form of Past.

1. buaileap.
2. buailip.
3. buaileapcap.

1. buailpeam or buailpiom.
2. buaileabap.
3. buailpeab, or buailpiob, or buailpeabap.

Consuetudinal Past

1. buailinn, I used to strike.
2. buailced, thou usedst to strike.
3. buaileab ré, he used to strike.

1. buailimíp, we used to strike.
2. buailcí, ye used to strike.
3. buailibíp, they used to strike.

Future.

1. buailpeab, I will strike.
2. buailpip, thou wilt strike.
3. buailpib ré, he will strike.

1. buailpimíb, we will strike.
2. buailpib, ye will strike.
3. buailpib, they will strike.

(*For the relative form of this tense, see p.* 55.)

CONDITIONAL MOOD.

1. buailpinn, I would strike.
2. buailped, thou wouldst strike.
3. buailpeab ré, he would strike.

1. buailpimíp, we would strike.
2. buailpib, ye would strike.
3. buailpibíp, they would strike.

INF. MOOD. Do bualab, *to strike.* PART. Aʒ bualab, *striking.*

PASSIVE VOICE.

IMPERATIVE MOOD.

(The same as the Indicative Present.)

INDICATIVE MOOD.

Present Tense.

Singular.
1. buailteaṗ mé, I am struck.
2. buailteaṗ tú, thou art struck.
3. buailteaṗ é, he is struck.

Plural.
1. buailteaṗ ṗinn or inn, we are struck.
2. buailteaṗ ṗiḃ or iḃ, ye are struck.
3. buailteaṗ iaḋ, they are struck.

Consuetudinal Present.

(Same as the Indicative Present.)

Past.

1. buaileaḋ mé, I was struck.
2. buaileaḋ tú, thou wast struck.
3. buaileaḋ é, he was struck.

1. buaileaḋ ṗinn or inn, we were struck.
2. buaileaḋ ṗiḃ or iḃ, ye were struck.
3. buaileaḋ iaḋ, they were struck.

Consuetudinal Past.

1. buailtí mé, I used to be struck.
2. buailtí tú, thou usedst to be struck.
3. buailtí é, he used to be struck.

1. buailtí ṗinn or inn, we used to be struck.
2. buailtí ṗiḃ or iḃ, ve used to be struck.
3. buailtí iaḋ, they used to be struck.

Future.

Singular.
1. buailfean mé, I shall or will be struck.
2. buailfean tú, thou shalt or wilt be struck.
3. buailfean é, he shall or will be struck.

Plural.
1. buailfean finn or inn, we shall or will be struck.
2. buailfean fib or ib, ye shall or will be struck.
3. buailfean iad, they shall or will be struck.

Conditional Mood.

1. buailfíðe mé, I would be struck.
2. buailfíðe tú, thou wouldst be struck.
3. buailfíðe é, he would be struck.

1. buailfíðe finn or inn, we would be struck.
2. buailfíðe fib or ib, ye would be struck.
3. buailfíðe iad, they would be struck.

Infinitive Mood.

Do beit buailte, *to be struck.*

Participle.

buailte, *struck.*

IV. RELATIVE FORM OF THE VERB.

1. Besides the forms given in the preceding conjugation, the verb has what is called a "relative form," i.e., a form used after a relative pronoun. In two of the tenses of the indicative mood, namely, the present and the future, the relative form has a distinct inflection, viz., af, if, eaf, or iof.

2. For instance, "the person who calls," is translated, not by an té a ġoifið (3rd sing. form), but by an té a ġoifeaf; and "he who will steal," is not an te a ġoiofið (3rd sing. form), but an té a ġoiofeaf. In other tenses and moods the relative form is the same as that of the third person singular.

3. This form of the verb is often used even when its nominative is not a relative, but a noun or personal pronoun, to express the "historical present," i.e., the present tense used for the past; as ꝑiaꝑꝑaiᵹeaꞃ Aiṁiꝛᵹiⁿ a h-aiɳim ꝺi, "Amergin *asks* her name of her." (See for a further account of the historical present, p. 57.)

4. And not unfrequently the relative form is used as an ordinary present; as, Iꞃ móꝛ an ꞇ-ionᵹna liomꞃa, naċ ꝺ'Oiꞃſín iaꝛꝛaꞃ Fionn miꞃe, "It is a great wonder to me that it is not for Oisin Finn *seeks* (iaꝛꝛaꞃ) me."

V. FORMATION AND USES OF THE MOODS AND TENSES OF REGULAR VERBS.

1. The second person singular of the imperative mood, active voice, is the root or simplest form of the verb, from which all the other persons, moods, and tenses are formed directly, by affixing the various terminations.

2. Verbs which end in a consonant preceded by a slender vowel have all their inflections precisely like those of buail (with the exception mentioned in Par. 4, p. 60); and they all begin with a slender vowel (except sometimes that of the infinitive) in accordance with the rule caol le caol &c.

3. But when the final consonant is preceded by a broad vowel, the synthetic terminations begin with a broad vowel, in accordance with the same rule. A table of the full conjugation of a regular verb ending in a broad vowel is given at page. 64.

4. The root generally remains unchanged through all the variations of the verb, except that it occasionally suffers a trifling change in the infinitive. The cases in which the root suffers change in the infinitive are mentioned in Par. 4. p. 60: See also Par. 8, p. 63.

Indicative Mood.

Present Tense.

1. The present tense is formed by affixing the six personal terminations ım (or aım), ır (or aır), &c., to the root.

2. The historical present, i.e., the present tense used for the past, or where past time is intended, is very common in Irish; indeed in many narrative and historical pieces it occurs quite as often as the ordinary past tense in relating past transactions; as, Ɗala lċ, ıomorro, ollṁuıġċear long leır, "as to Ith, indeed, a ship *is prepared* by him" (instead of ollṁuıġeaḋ, *was prepared*).

3. It has been already remarked (Par. 3, p. 56), that the relative form of the verb is often used for the historical present; as noċtar Eıreṁón ḋóıḃ, "Eremon reveals to them."

Consuetudinal Past and Present.

1. These tenses express customary action; as léıġeann mé, I am in the habit of reading; léıġeaḋ ré, he used to read, or he was in the habit of reading.

2. In the sentences, "I write always after breakfast," and "he sold bread in his youth," the verbs "write" and "sold" are used in the same manner as the Irish consuetudinal tense; except, indeed, that the idea is not so distinctly marked by the English phrase as by the Irish.

3. One of the particles ɗo or ro is usually prefixed to the consuetudinal past; and the initial consonant is generally aspirated; as do ᵹoıpıðíp, they used to call.

4. The Irish peasantry seem to feel the want of these two tenses when they are speaking English; and they often, in fact, attempt to import them into the English language, even in districts where no Irish has been spoken for generations: thus they will say, " I do be reading while you do be writing;" "I used to be walking every day while I lived in the country," &c.

Past Tense.

1. In the past tense the initial consonant is aspirated in the active voice, but not in the passive voice.

2. With the exception of the aspiration, the third singular past tense is the same as the root.

3. One of the particles do or po is generally prefixed to the past tense in both voices; as do ṗeapap, I stood; po ċoolaıp, thou sleepedst; do molað ıað, they were praised; po buaıleað ó, he was struck.

4. The particle po, used as a mark of the past tense, is often compounded with other particles, the p only being retained, but it still causes aspiration in the active voice, as if it were uncompounded.

5. The principal of these compounds are:—

(1.) Ap, whether? from an and po; as ap buaıl ṗé, did he strike?

(2.) ᵹup, that, from ᵹo and po; as cpeıoım ᵹup buaıl ṗé, I believe that he struck.

(3.) Munap, unless, from muna and po; as munap buaıl ṗé, unless he struck.

(4.) Naċap, or na'p, or náp, whether not? from naċ and po; as náp buaıl ṗé, did not he strike?

(5.) Níop, not, from ní and po; as níop buail ré, he did not strike.*

6. The particle po, as a sign of past tense, is also often combined with the relative pronoun a; as an peap d'ap ʒeallap mo leabap, the man *to whom* I promised my book. For a further account of this, see Syntax.

Future Tense.

1. All the personal inflections of this tense, in both voices, begin with the letter p, which, in the spoken language, is often sounded like h; thus dúnpad, I shall shut, is colloquially pronounced *doonhad* (instead of *doonfad*).

Conditional Mood.

1. The particle do, causing aspiration, is often prefixed to verbs in the conditional mood; as do ṗiubalpainn, I would walk.

2. But very often also dá, if, or muna, unless, is prefixed, and with these particles the initial is eclipsed; as dá b-paʒainn-pe mo poʒa, "if I would get my choice;" muna m-beiðead pé, "unless he would be."

3. It is important to note that the personal inflections of this mood in both voices, as well as those of the future indicative, all begin with p.

Infinitive Mood.

1. The initial is aspirated in the infinitive, whether the particle do or a be expressed or under-

---

* See Second Irish Book by the Society for the Preservation of the Irish Language, p. 53.

stood. But in some cases the aspiration is prevented by other grammatical influences, as shown in next paragraph.

2. When the infinitive is preceded by one of the possessive pronouns, the initial of the verb falls under the influence of the pronoun.*

(1.) It is aspirated for a, his; mo, my; do, thy (but here the influence of the pronoun is not perceived, as there would be aspiration without it); as dá ġonaḋ, to wound him (literally to his wounding, and so of the others); do m'ġonaḋ, to wound me; do d'ġonaḋ, to wound thee.

(2.) It is preserved from aspiration by a, her; as dá ġonaḋ, to wound her.

(3.) It is eclipsed by the three plural possessives; as dáp n-ġonaḋ, to wound us; do ḃup n-ġonaḋ to wound you; dá n-ġonaḋ, to wound them.

3. The general way of forming the infinitive is by adding aḋ or eaḋ, the first when the last vowel of the root is broad; the second when the vowel is slender.

4. If the final consonant of the root be preceded by ı as part of a diphthong or triphthong, the final vowel is made broad in the infinitive (which is usually, but not always, done by dropping the ı); as buaıl, bualaḋ; ġoın, ġonaḋ, to wound. But if the final consonant be preceded by ı alone, the infinitive is formed according to the general rule in the last paragraph; as mıll, mılleaḋ, to destroy.

5. The infinitives of many verbs are formed irregularly, and these must be learned by prac-

* For the influence of the possessive pronouns, see pages 9, 11, 12; and see also Syntax.

tice. The following are a few of such verbs. Each group exhibits a particular type, in which the manner of forming the infinitive will be obvious on inspection.

Root or Imperative.	Infinitive.
éaʒ.	b'éaʒ, to die.
ṗnáṁ.	bo ṗnáṁ, to swim.
ól.	b'ól, to drink.
ταρρaιnʒ.	bo ταρρaιnʒ, to draw.
cuιρ.	bo ċuρ, to put.
ʒοιl.	bo ʒοl, to weep.
ιmιρ.	b'ιmιρτ, to play.
ιnġιl.	b'ιnġιlτ, to graze.
bíbιρ.	bo bíbιρτ, to banish.
ceιl.	bo ċeιlτ, to conceal.
ḟáʒ.	b' ḟáʒbáιl, to leave.
ʒaḃ.	bo ʒaḃáιl, to take.
τόʒ.	bo τόʒbáιl, to lift.
lean.	bo leanaṁaιn, to follow.
caιll.	bo ċaιlleaṁaιn, to lose.
oιl.	b'oιleaṁaιn, to nourish.
ḟoιll.	b'ḟoιlleaṁaιn to suit.
ʒluaιρ.	bo ʒluaρaċτ, to move.
éιρτ.	b'éιρτeaċτ, to listen.

The Participle.

1. The active participle is merely the infinitive mood, with some such particle as aʒ prefixed; as aʒ bualaḋ at beating or a-beating.

2. The passive participle is generally formed by adding τe or ċe when the last vowel of the root is slender, and τa or ċa, when broad.

When the root ends in ċ, ḃ, l, ll, n, nn, ρ, ċ, or ġ (except verbs in uιġ or ιġ), the τ of the participial termination retains its sound: after any other consonant, and also in verbs in uιġ or ιġ, the τ is aspirated. In the passive voice, the terminations ταρ and τí follow the same law.

VI. VERBS IN uiġ, &c.

1. Verbs of two or more syllables with the root ending in uiġ, or iġ, and some other dissyllabic verbs ending in il, ın, ıp, and ır, differ so decidedly from the model verb in the formation of some of their moods and tenses, that some writers,* not without reason, class them as a second conjugation.

2. The difference lies in the formation of the future and of the conditional in both voices; the other moods and tenses are formed like those of buail.

3. In buail, and all other verbs of its kind, the letter p is a characteristic mark of the future and of the conditional mood in both voices, as stated in Par. 3, p. 59.

4. The verbs now under consideration have no p in the future and conditional, but they take instead, eó, before the final consonant of the root.

5. In addition to this change, verbs in uiġ and iġ change ġ into c; though in the spoken language of most parts of Ireland, the ġ retains its place.

6. There is no other inflectional difference between these verbs and buail, the personal terminations following the final consonant of the root being the same in all cases.

7. In the other tenses of the indicative, verbs in il, ın, ıp and ır are almost always syncopated by the elision of the vowel or diphthong preceding the final root consonant, as codail, sleep, codlaim,

---

* As for instance the Rev. Canon Bourke in his "College Irish Grammar."

I sleep, &c. (But this change is not regarded as grammatical inflection.)

8. Verbs in uiġ almost always form their infinitive by dropping the i and adding the usual termination aḋ; those in iġ alone (not preceded by u), retain the i and take u after it in the infinitive: as comarċuiġ, mark; infinitive, comarċuġaḋ; comairliġ, advise; infinitive, comairliuġaḋ.

9. Sometimes there are other slight changes, caused chiefly by the rule caol le caol &c., which will be obvious on inspection.

10. The following are a few examples of the formation of the present and future indicative, and of the conditional mood, in such verbs. The first person singular only is given in each case, as the other persons have the same terminations as buail and meall.

Root or imper.	Pres. indic.	Future indic.	Conditional Mood.
Díriġ, direct.	díriġim.	díreóċaḋ.	díreóċainn.
Gráḋuiġ, love.	gráḋuiġim.	gráḋóċaḋ.	gráḋóċainn.
Labair, speak.	labraim.	laibeórad.	laibeórainn.
Tarruing. draw.	tairngim.	tairreóngaḋ.	tairreóngainn.
Forgail, open.	forglaim.	foirgeólaḋ.	foirgeólainn.
Cosain. defend.	cosnaim.	coiseónaḋ.	coiseónainn.
Innis, tell,	innisim.	inneósaḋ.	inneósainn.
Díbir, banish.	díbrim.	díbeóraḋ.	díbeórainn.

11. In Munster, verbs in il, in, ir, and is, are conjugated like those in uiġ or iġ; and the eó comes *after* the final consonant: thus díbir, banish, is made in the future and conditional, díbreóċaḋ and díbreóċainn, as if the verb were díbriġ.

12. A table of the full conjugation of a verb in uiġ (áḋbuiġ) is given at page 65

Synthetic Conjugation of meall, deceive.

	Active Voice		Passive Voice	
	Singular	Plural	Singular	Plural
Imperative Mood	1. — 2. meall 3. meall-aḋ ré	meall-amaoir meall-aiḋ meall-aoir	Same form as the Present Indicative.	
Indicative Mood — Pres. Tense	1. meall-aim 2. meall-air 3. meall-aḋ ré	meall-amaoid meall-taoi meall-aid	meall-tar {mé, tú, é}	meall-tar {rinn, inn riḃ, iḃ iad}
Consuet. Present	1. meall- {ann} 2. meall- {ann} 3. meall- {ré}	meall-ann {rinn riḃ riad}	Same form as the Present.	
Simple Past	1. ṁeall-ar 2. ṁeall-air 3. ṁeall ré	ṁeall-amar ṁeall-aḃar ṁeall-aḋar	meall-aḋ {mé, tú, é}	meall-aḋ {rinn, inn riḃ, iḃ iad}
Consuet. Past	1. ṁeall-ainn 2. ṁeall-tá 3. ṁeall-aḋ ré	ṁeall-amaoir ṁeall-taoi ṁeall-aoir	meall-taoi {mé, tú, é}	meall-taoi {rinn, inn riḃ, iḃ iad}
Future	1. meall-faḋ 2. meall-fair 3. meall-faiḋ ré	meall-famaoid meall-faiḋ meall-faid	meall-far {mé, tú, é}	meall-far {rinn, inn riḃ, iḃ iad}
Conditional Mood	1. ṁeall-fainn 2. meall-fá 3. ṁeall-faḋ ré	ṁeall-famaoir ṁeall-faḋ ṁeall-faḋaoir	ṁeall-faiḋe {mé, tú, é}	meall-faiḋe {rinn, inn riḃ, iḃ iad}
Infinitive Mood, do ṁeall-aḋ.			Infinitive Mood, do beiṫ meall-ta.	
Participle, aġ meall-aḋ.			Participle, meall-ta.	

THE VERB.

SYNTHETIC CONJUGATION OF árouiġ, raise.

		ACTIVE VOICE		PASSIVE VOICE	
		SINGULAR	PLURAL	SINGULAR	PLURAL
Imperative Mood.	1.	—	árouiġ-mís	Same form as the Present Indicative.	
	2.	árouiġ	árouiġ-íó		
	3.	árouiġ-eaó ré	árouiġ-óís		
Indicative Mood — Pres. Tense.	1.	árouiġ-im	árouiġ-mío	árouiġ-tear { mé, tú, é }	árouiġ-tear { rinn, mn, ríb, íb, íao }
	2.	árouiġ-ir	árouiġ-tí		
	3.	árouiġ-íó ré	árouiġ-ío		
Consuet. Present.	1.	árouiġ-eann { mé, tú, ré }	árouiġ-eann { rinn, ríb, íao }	Same form as the Present.	
	2.				
	3.				
Simple Past.	1.	árouiġ-ear	árouiġ-eamar	árouiġ-eaó { mé, tú, é }	árouiġ-eaó { rinn, mn, ríb, íb, íao }
	2.	árouiġ-ir	árouiġ-eaóar		
	3.	árouiġ ré	árouiġ-eaóar		
Consuet. Past.	1.	árouiġ-inn	árouiġ-mír	árouiġ-tí { mé, tú, é }	árouiġ-tí { rinn, mn, ríb, íb, íao }
	2.	árouiġ-teá	árouiġ tí		
	3.	árouiġ-eaó ré	árouiġ-óír		
Future.	1.	áiroeóc-ao	áiroeóc-amaoir	áiroeóc-ar { mé, tú, é }	áiroeóc-ar { rinn, mn, ríb, íb, íao }
	2.	áiroeóc-air	áiroeóc-taoió		
	3.	áiroeóc-aó ré	áiroeóc-aio		
Conditional Mood.	1.	áiroeóc-ainn	áiroeóc-amaoír	áiroeóc-aíóe { mé, tú, é }	áiroeóc-aíóe { rinn, mn, ríb, íb, íao }
	2.	áiroeóc-tá	áiroeóc-taoió		
	3.	áiroeóc-aó ré	áiroeóc-aíoír		

Infinitive Mood, o'áirouġaó.
Participle, aġ ároúġaó.

Infinitive Mood, ío beit áirouiġte.
Participle, áirouiġte.

VII. IRREGULAR VERBS.

1. There are fourteen irregular verbs, several of which are defective, i.e., want one or more of the moods and tenses. The conjugation of some of them, it will be observed, is made up of that of two or more different verbs.

2. It will also be observed that through all their irregularities, the five synthetic personal terminations remain unchanged; for which reason it is scarcely correct to call these verbs irregular at all.

3. The irregular verbs are as follows:—(1), táim, I am; (2), the assertive verb ip; (3), beipim, I give; (4), beipim, I bear; (5), cím, I see (including peicim); (6), cluinim, I hear; (7), déanaim, I do; (8), gním or ním, I do; (9), beipim, I say; (10), pagaim or geibim, I find; (11), itim, I eat; (12), pigim, I reach; (13), téidim, I go; (14), tigim, I come.

4. The following is the synthetic conjugation of the irregular verbs (except in the case of the second verb ip, which has no synthetic conjugation). They may be all conjugated analytically, by using the third person singular of each tense with the three personal pronouns singular and plural, as shown in case of the regular verb at page 49. As an example, the analytic conjugation of the present tense of the first verb, táim, is given.

(1.) Táim, *I am.*

IMPERATIVE MOOD.

Singular.
1. . . . .
2. bí, be thou.
3. bíocað ré, or bíoñ ré, let him be.

Plural.
1. bímíp, let us be.
2. bíðíð, be ye.
3. bíðíp, let them be.

THE VERB.

Indicative Mood.

Present Tense.

Singular.
1. táim, atáim, I am.
2. táir, atáir, thou art.
3. tá ré, atá ré, he is.

Plural.
1. támaoid, atámaoid, we are.
2. tátaoi, atátaoi, ye are.
3. táid, atáid, they are.

Present Tense: analytic conjugation.

1. tá mé, atá mé, I am.
2. tá tú, atá tú, thou art.
3. tá ré, atá ré, he is.

1. tá rinn, atá rinn, we are.
2. tá rib, atá rib, ye are.
3. tá riad, atá riad, they are.

Consuetudinal Present.

1. bídim, I am usually.
2. bídir, thou art usually.
3. bídeann ré, or bíonn ré, he is usually.

1. bímíd, bídmíd, bíomaoid, we are usually.
2. bítí, bídtí, ye are usually.
3. bíd, bídid, they are usually.

Interrogative and Negative Present.

(The negative particle is here used: see Par. 3, p. 69.)

1. ní b-fuilim, I am not.*
2. ní b-fuilir, thou art not.
3. ní b-fuil ré, he is not.

1. ní b-fuilmíd, we are not.
2. ní b-fuiltí, ye are not.
3. ní b-fuilid, they are not.

---

* These are commonly pronounced in conversation as if the b-fu were omitted in each case; and accordingly they are often contracted in books to nf'lim, nf'lir, nfl ré, &c.

68   ETYMOLOGY.   [PART

Past Tense.

Singular.
1. bíḋeap, bíop, I was.
2. bíḋip, bíp, thou wert.
3. bíḋ ṗé, bí ṗé, he was.

Plural.
1. bíḋeamap, bíomap, we were.
2. bíḋeaḃap, bíoḃap, ye were.
3. bíḋeaḃap, bíoḃap, they were.

Consuetudinal Past.

1. bíḋinn, bínn, I used to be.
2. bíḋċeá, bíċeá, thou usedst to be.
3. bíḋeaḋ ṗé, bíoḋ ṗé, he used to be.

1. bíḋmíṗ, bímíṗ, we used to be.
2. bíḋċí, bíċí, ye used to be.
3. bíḋḋíṗ, bíḋíṗ, they used to be.

Interrogative and Negative Past.

(The negative particle is here used: see Par. 3, p. 69).

1. ní paḃap, I was not.
2. ní paḃaip, thou wert not.
3. ní paiḃ ṗé, he was not.

1. ní paḃamap, we were not.
2. ní paḃaḃap, ye were not.
3. ní paḃaḃap, they were not.

Future.

1. beiḋeaḋ, I shall be.
2. beiḋip, thou shalt be.
3. beiḋ ṗé, he shall be.

1. beiḋmíḋ, we shall be.
2. beiḋiḋ, ye shall be.
3. beiḋiḋ, they shall be.

Conditional Mood.

1. beiḋinn, I would be.
2. beiḋteá, thou wouldst be.
3. beiḋeaḋ ré, or beiṫ ré, he would be.

1. beiḋmír, we would be.
2. beiḋtí, ye would be.
3. beiḋír, they would be.

Infinitive Mood.

Do beiṫ, *to be.*

Participle.

Aġ beiṫ, *being.*

1. Tá is commonly called the substantive verb, and answers to the verb " to be" in English.

2. It has two forms, which the regular verb has not, namely, a form in the present tense for interrogation and negation (b-ḟuilim), and a form in the past tense for the same (raḃar). These two are classed by O'Donovan as a subjunctive mood, present and past tense.

3. The forms b-ḟuilim and raḃar are used only:—

(*a.*) After negative and interrogative particles; as ní b-ḟuil ré tinn, he is not sick; ní raiḃ mé ann rin, I was not there: an b-ḟuil ḟíon in ḃar lonġaiḃ? "Is there wine in your ships?" An raḃair aġ an ġ-carraiġ? "Wert thou at the rock" (or at Carrick)? O naċ b-ḟuil ḋul uaiḃ aġam, "since I cannot escape from him" (lit. "since it is not with me to go from him"); an b-ḟuil a ḟior aġat féin, a Ḟinn? ní ḟuil, ar Fionn, "'Is the knowledge of it with thyself, O Finn?' 'It is not,' says Finn."

(But these forms are not used after the interrogative cionnar, how?)

(*b.*) After ᵹo, *that*; as ḃeıpım ᵹo ḃ-ḟuıl ṗé ṗlán, I say that he is well.

(*c.*) After the relative a when it follows a preposition, or when it signifies "all that" (Par. 3, page 47); as cpeuḃ ó an ḟpeaᵹpa ċaḃappaıp ap Ṫhıa, aᵹ a ḃ-ḟuıl ḟıop ḃo loċt? "What answer wilt thou give to God, who has a knowledge of thy sins?" (lit. "*with whom* is a knowledge"); a ḃ-ḟuıl ó Áṫ-clıaṫ ᵹo h-Oıleán móp an Ḃhappaıᵹ, "*all that* is from Ath-cliath (Dublin) to Oileán mór an Bharraigh;" ḃo ḃeıpmıṡ ap m-ḃpıaṫap naċ beaᵹ lınn a m-beupam ᵹo Ḟıonn ḋıoḃ, "we pledge our word, that we do not think it little, *all that* we shall bring of them to Finn."

4. This verb, like verbs in general, has a relative form for the present and future; but the relative form of the present is always a consuetudinal tense (whereas in regular verbs it is generally not consuetudinal); as map an ᵹ-céaḋna ḃíoṗ (or ḃíḋeap) an báp an oıpċıll ḃo ṗíop ap an ḃuıne; "in like manner death is (in the habit of) lying in wait always for man."

5. The analytic form of this verb is now far more common in the spoken language than the synthetic. In asking a question the analytic form is often preferred: but in answering, the synthetic; as an paıḃ tú aᵹ an ᵹ-Cappaıᵹ? Ḋo ḃíop aᵹ an ᵹ-Cappaıᵹ, "Were you at Carrick? I was at Carrick."

6. The letter a is often prefixed to the present tense both in speaking and writing: atá instead of tá, &c.; it is sometimes slightly emphatic, but oftener merely euphonic, and does not otherwise affect the meaning.

7. This verb is often used as an auxiliary, like the verb "to be" in English; and it is the only verb in the Irish language that can be regarded as an auxiliary. Thus, instead of buɑılceɑɲ mé, I am struck, we can say cá mé buɑılce: for do buɑıleɑð mé, I was struck, do bí mé buɑılce, &c.

(2.) Iɼ, *it is.*

INDICATIVE MOOD.

Present Tense.

Iɼ, it is: as ıɼ mé, it is I; ıɼ cú, it is thou.

Past Tense.

bɑ or buð, it was; as bɑ mé, it was I.

Future Tense.

buð o. buɼ, it will be.

CONDITIONAL MOOD.

bɑð, it would be,

1. This is commonly called the assertive verb.

2. It has no inflection for person, being always used in the third person singular: hence it is often called the impersonal verb.

3. It has no other moods and tenses besides those given above.

4. It takes other forms in the modern language, some of them contracted, which are often puzzling to learners.

5. After ɡuɼ, that, it is often made ɑb, which is given by O'Donovan as a subjunctive mood; as cɼeıðım ɡuɼ ɑb é ɑcá cınn, I believe that it is he (who) is sick: meɑɼuım ðá péıɼ ɼın, ɡuɼ ɑb ðá bhɑɡɑın ɑɡuɼ ғıċe ɼul ɼuɡɑð Abɼɑhɑm cáınıc Pɑɼċolón ı n-Eıɼınn, "I think, according to that

that it is two years and twenty before Abraham was born, that Partholon came to Erin."

6. Very often ɼup ab is shortened by omitting the a; as cpeıoım ɼup 'bé, &c.; and sometimes the b is joined to ɼup, as cpeıoım ɼupb é, &c.

7. After má, if, the ı is omitted, as má'ɼ pɼoṅ é. if it be true; and in this case the ɼ is often joined to the má; as máɼ pɼoṅ é: máɼ maıṫ leaṫ a beıṫ buan, caıṫ puap aɼup ṫeıṫ, "if you wish to be long-lived, drink cold and hot" (or "drink cold and flee"—a celebrated Irish saying of double meaning).

8. Sometimes ba or ḃa is shortened to b or ḃ alone, which again is often joined to the preceding word; as laoċ ḃ'áp ḃ'aınm Lıp, or laoċ ḃapḃ aınm Lıp, "a hero whose name was Lir;" of which the full construction is, laoċ ḃo a ɼo ḃa aınm Lıp, "a hero to whom was name Lir."

9. There is another form, pá, for the past tense, which is now disused, but which is constantly used by Keating, and by other writers of the seventeenth and eighteenth centuries: pá ṫɼéanpeap an Ceaṫ ɼo, "this Ceat was a mighty man;" ıɼ í (banba) pa bean ḃo Mhac Coıll, ḃ'aɼ ḃ'aınm ḃílıoɼ Eaṫúp, "it is she (Banba) who was wife to Mac Coll, whose proper name was Eathur;" óɼ é an ɼcoıṫḃéapla pá ṫeanɼa coıṫċeann ɼan Scıṫıa an ṫpáṫ ḃo ṫpıall Neıṁeaḋ aıpḃe, "since it is the Scotic language which was the common tongue in Scythia in the time that Neimheadh emigrated from it."*

10. For the distinction between ṫá and ıɼ, see Idioms.

---

* For the various forms assumed by this verb in the ancient language, see O'Donovan's most instructive article in his "Irish Grammar," p. 161.

CHAP. V.] THE VERB. 73

(3.) bheipim, *I give.*

ACTIVE VOICE.

IMPERATIVE MOOD.

Singular.   Plural.
1. . . .   1. ꞇabpamaoıp.
2. ꞇabaıp.   2. ꞇabpaıꝺ.
3. ꞇabpaꝺ ꞅé.   3. ꞇabpaꝺaoıp.

INDICATIVE MOOD.

First Person Singular.

Present : beıpım, ꞇabpaım, or
          ꞇuɜaım.
Consuet. Pres.: beıpeann.
Past : ꞇuɜap.
Consuet. Past : beıpınn, ꞇuɜaınn.
Future : béappaꝺ, ꞇabappaꝺ.

} With the usual terminations for the other persons and numbers.

CONDITIONAL béappaınn, ꞇabappaınn.
MOOD :

INFINITIVE; ꝺo ꞇabaıpꞇ. PARTICIPLE; aɜ ꞇabaıpꞇ.

PASSIVE VOICE.

IMPERATIVE; beıpꞇeap, ꞇabapꞇap, ꞇuɜꞇap, mé, ꞇú, é, &c.

INDICATIVE MOOD.

Present : beıpꞇeap, ꞇuɜꞇap.
Past : ꞇuɜaꝺ.
Consuet. Past : beıpꞇıꝺe, ꞇuɜꞇaıꝺe.
Future : béappap, ꞇabappap.

CONDITIONAL béappaıꝺe, ꞇabappaıꝺe.
MOOD :

} mé, ꞇú, é, &c.

INFINITIVE; ꝺo beıꞇ ꞇabapꞇa, ꝺo beıꞇ ꞇuɜꞇa.
PARTICIPLE; ꞇabapꞇa, ꞇuɜꞇa.

1. This verb is made up of three different verbs: in some of the tenses any one of the three may be employed; in some, either of two; and in some only one; as shown in the paradigm.

2. In the present tense, beiṗim (but not the other two verbs) takes the particle do (which is a mark of the past in regular verbs), and commonly has its initial aspirated.

(4.) beiṗim, *I bear.*

ACTIVE VOICE.

Imperative Mood.

Singular.	Plural.
1. . . .	1. beiṗimíṗ.
2. beiṗ.	2. beiṗiḋ.
3. beiṗeaḋ ṗé.	3. beiṗiḋíṗ.

Indicative Mood.

First Person Singular.

Present:	beiṗim.	⎫
Consuet. Present:	beiṗeann.	⎪ With the usual
Past:	ṗuġaṗ.	⎬ terminations for
Consuet. Past:	beiṗinn.	⎪ the other persons
Future:	béaṗṗaḋ.	⎪ and numbers.
Conditional Mood:	ḃéaṗṗainn.	⎭

Infinitive; do ḃṗeiṫ.   Participle; aġ ḃṗeiṫ.

PASSIVE VOICE.

Imperative Mood; beiṗteaṗ mé, tú, é, &c.

THE VERB.

Indicative Mood.

Present:	beirτeaρ.	
Past:	ρυζαὸ.	
Consuet. Past:	bcirτí.	⎫ mé, τú, é, &c.
Future:	béaρρar.	⎬
Conditional Mood:	béaρρaιὸc	⎭

Infinitive; ὸo beιτ beιrτe   Participle; beιrτe.

(5.) Cím, *I see*.

ACTIVE VOICE.

Imperative Mood.

Singular.
1. . . .
2. ρeιc
3. ρeιceaὸ ρé.

Plural.
1. ρeιcιmír, ρeιcιmfò.
2. ρeιcíò.
3. ρeιcιòír.

Indicative Mood.

Present Tense.

1. cíòιm, cím, ρeιcιm.
2. cíòιr. cír, ρeιcιr.
3. cíòιò ρé, cιò ρé, ρeιcιò ρé.

1. cíòmfò, címfò, ρeιcιmfò
2. cíbcí, cící, ρeιccí.
3. cíòιò, cíò, ρeιcιò.

Consuet. Pres.; cíòeann, ρeιceann, mé, τú, ρé, &c.

Past.

1. connaρcaρ.
2. connaρcaιρ
3. connaιρc ρé.

1. concamaρ.
2. concaban.
3. concaban.

First Person Singular.

Consuet. Past:	cíòιnn or cínn.	⎫ With the usual terminations for the other persons and numbers.
Future:	cíòρeaò or cíρeaò.	⎬
Conditional Mood:	cíòριnn, or círιnn, or ρeιcριnn.	⎭

Infinitive Mood; ὸ'ρeιcrιn or ὸ'ρeιcrιnτ.
Participle; aζ ρeιcrιn or aζ ρeιcrιnτ.

PASSIVE VOICE.

IMPERATIVE MOOD; peictear, mé, tú, é, &c.

INDICATIVE MOOD.

Present Tense: cíoccap or peicceap.
Past: connapcaó.
Past. Consuet.: cíbtí or pcictí.
Future: cíopean or peicpean. } mé, tú, é, &c.

CONDITIONAL cíopide or pcicpide.
MOOD :

INFINITIVE MOOD; bo beit peicte.   PARTICIPLE; peicte

1. Cíoim is defective in some of its moods and tenses, which are supplied by other verbs—the imperative and infinitive by peicim or paicim, and the past indicative of both voices by an old verb—otherwise disused—connapcaim.

2. Peicim or paicim, although it is brought in among the irregular verbs to supply the defects of cíoim, is itself regular.

3. Observe that the initial of cíoim is *always* aspirated.

(6.) Cluinim. *I hear.*

INDICATIVE MOOD.

Past Tense.

1. cualar.
2. cualair.
3. cualaió ré.

1. cualamap.
2. cualabap.
3. cualabap.

INFINITIVE MOOD ACTIVE; bo clop or bo cloiptin.

PARTICIPLE ACTIVE ; ag clop or ag cloiptin.

1. In all the other moods and tenses, cluinim is regular, and is conjugated like buail.

(**7.**) ḋéanaim, *I do.*

ACTIVE VOICE.

IMPERATIVE MOOD.

1. . . .   1. ḋéanam, ḋéanamaoir,
                                         ḋéanamaoiḋ.
2. ḋéan.   2. ḋéanaiḋ.
3. ḋéanaḋ ré.   3. ḋéanaiḋír.

INDICATIVE MOOD.

Past Tense.

1. riġnear, ḋeárnar, ḋéa-   1. riġneamar, ḋeárnamar,
   nar.   ḋéanamar.
2. riġnir, ḋeárnair, ḋéa-   2. riġneaḋar, ḋeárnaḋar,
   nair.   ḋéanaḋar.
3. riġne ré, ḋeárnaḋ ré,   3. riġneaḋar, ḋeárnaḋar,
   ḋéan ré.   ḋéanaḋar.

First Person Singular.

Present : ḋéanaim.
Consuet. Pres. : ḋéanann.
Consuet. Past : ġníoinn, ḋearnainn, ḋéa-   With the
   nainn.   usual termina-
Future : ḋéanraḋ.   tions for the
                                                                            other persons
CONDITIONAL ḋéanrainn.   and numbers.
MOOD :

INFINITIVE MOOD ; do ḋéanaṁ or do ḋéanaḋ.
PARTICIPLE ; aġ ḋéanaṁ or aġ ḋéanaḋ.

PASSIVE VOICE.

IMPERATIVE MOOD ; Ḋéantar mé, tú, é, &c.

INDICATIVE MOOD.

Present : ḋéantar.
Past : riġneaḋ, ḋeárnaḋ.
Consuet. Past : ġnítí.   mé, tú, é, &c.
Future : ḋéanrar.

CONDITIONAL ḋéanraiḋe.
MOOD :

INFINITIVE MOOD ; do ḃeit ḋéanta. PARTICIPLE ; ḋéanta.

1. This verb and the next borrow from each other to form some of the moods and tenses in which they are defective.

(8.) ᵹním or ním, *I do.*

ACTIVE VOICE.

INDICATIVE MOOD.

First Person Singular.

Present :   ᵹním or ním.
Past :   ᵹníḋear or níḋear.
Consuet. Past :   ᵹníḋinn or níḋinn.

} With the usual terminations for the other persons and numbers.

PASSIVE VOICE.

INDICATIVE MOOD.

Present :   ᵹníṫear or níṫear.
Consuet. Past : ᵹníṫí or níṫí.

} mé, tú, é, &c.

1. This verb is used in no other moods or tenses; but so far as it goes it is very common in both forms—with and without the ᵹ (ᵹním and ním). The other moods and tenses are expressed by means of déanaim.

(9.) deirim, *I say.*

ACTIVE VOICE.

IMPERATIVE MOOD.

Singular.	Plural.
1. . . .	1. abram, abramaoir, abramaoid.
2. abair.	2. abraid.
3. abrad ré:	3. abradaoir.

INDICATIVE MOOD.

Present Tense.

1. deirim:	1. deirimíd.
2. deirir.	2. deirtid
3. deir ré.	3. deirid.

Consuet. Pres. deireann me, tú, ré, &c.

Past.

1. dubṗaṗ.
2. dubṗaiṗ.
3. dubaiṗc ṗé.

1. dubṗamaṗ.
2. dubṗadaṗ.
3. dubṗadaṗ.

First Person Singular

Consuet. Past : deiṗinn.
Future : déaṗṗad.

Conditional Mood : déaṗṗainn.

} With the usual terminations for the other persons and numbers.

Infinitive Mood ; do ṗáḋ.   Participle ; aġ ṗáḋ.

PASSIVE VOICE.

Imperative Mood ; abaṗċaṗ mé, cú, é, &c.

Indicative Mood.

Present : deiṗċeaṗ.
Past : dubṗaḋ.
Consuet Past : deiṗċí.
Future : déaṗṗaṗ.

Conditional Mood : déaṗṗaide.

} mé, cú, é, &c.

Infinitive Mood ; do beiċ ṗáiḋce, do beiċ ṗáice.

Participle ; ṗáiḋce, ṗáice.

1. The verb abṗaim, I say, from which deiṗim borrows its imperative, is itself a regular verb.
2. Observe the characteristics of dubṗaṗ, the past indicative active :—(*a*) it does not take the participle do or ṗo ; (*b*) the initial is not aspirated.
3. The letter a is often prefixed to this verb for the sake of emphasis ; as a deiṗim for deiṗim, I say ; a dubaiṗc ṗé for dubaiṗc ṗé, he said.

(**10.**) ꝼᴀᵹᴀɪᴍ or ᵹᴇɪᴠɪᴍ, *I find.*

ACTIVE VOICE.
IMPERATIVE MOOD.

Singular.
1. . . .
2. ꝼᴀᵹ.
3. ꝼᴀᵹᴀᴠ, ꞅᴇ́.

Plural.
1. ꝼᴀᵹᴍᴀᴏɪꞅ, ꝼᴀᵹᴍᴀᴏɪᴠ.
2. ꝼᴀᵹᴀɪᴠ.
3. ꝼᴀᵹᴀɪᴠɪꞅ.

INDICATIVE MOOD.

Present Tense.

1. ꝼᴀᵹᴀɪᴍ or ᵹᴇɪᴠɪᴍ.
2. ꝼᴀᵹᴜɪꞃ or ᵹᴇɪᴠɪꞃ.
3. ꝼᴀᵹᴀɪᴠ ꞅᴇ́, or ᵹᴇɪᴠ ꞅᴇ́.

1. ꝼᴀᵹᴍᴀᴏɪᴠ or ᵹᴇɪᴠᴍɪᴠ.
2. ꝼᴀᵹᴛᴀɪᴠ or ᵹᴇɪᴠᴛɪᴠ.
3. ꝼᴀᵹᴀɪᴠ or ᵹᴇɪᴠɪᴠ.

Past.

1. ꝼᴜᴀꞃᴀꞅ.
2. ꝼᴜᴀꞃᴀɪꞅ.
3. ꝼᴜᴀɪꞃ ꞅᴇ́.

1. ꝼᴜᴀꞃᴀᴍᴀꞃ.
2. ꝼᴜᴀꞃᴀᴠᴀꞃ.
3. ꝼᴜᴀꞃᴀᴠᴀꞃ.

First Person Singular.

Consuet. Past :	ꝼᴀᵹᴀɪꞃꞃ or ᵹᴇɪᴠɪꞃꞃ.	With the usual terminations for the other persons and numbers.
Future :	ᵹᴇ́ᴀᴠᴀᴠ, ᵹᴇᴏᴠᴀᴠ.	
Future neg. & interrog.	ᵹᴇᴀᴠᴀᴠ or ᴠꝼᴜɪᵹᴇᴀᴠ.	
CONDITIONAL MOOD :	ᵹᴇ́ᴀᴠᴀɪꞃꞃ, ᵹᴇᴏᴠᴀɪꞃꞃ. or ᴠ-ꝼᴀᵹᴀɪꞃꞃ, ᴠ-ꝼᴜɪᵹɪꞃꞃ	

INFINITIVE; ᴠ'ꝼᴀ́ᵹᴀɪʟ. PARTICIPLE; ᴀᵹ ꝼᴀ́ᵹᴀɪʟ.

PASSIVE VOICE.
IMPERATIVE MOOD; ꝼᴀᵹᴛᴀꞃ me, ᴛᴜ́, ᴇ, &c.

INDICATIVE MOOD.

Present :	ꝼᴀᵹᴛᴀꞃ.	
Past :	ꝼᴜᴀꞃᴀᴠ or ꝼꞃɪᴛ.	mᴇ, ᴛᴜ, ᴇ. &c.
Consuet. Past :	ᵹᴇɪᴠᴛɪ.	
CONDITIONAL MOOD :	ᵹᴇᴀᴠᴛᴀɪᴠᴇ, ᴠ-ꝼᴜɪᵹᴛɪᴠᴇ.	

(*Defective in Infinitive and Participle.*)

THE VERB.

1. The second form of this verb (ɥeıƀım) has its initial aspirated in the present and future active.

2. The past tense (ꝼuapap, &c.) may or may not take the particle do or po ; but its initial consonant is not aspirated.

(11.) lċım, *I eat.*

ACTIVE VOICE.

First Person Singular.

Future Indicative : ıoꝼꝼaḋ.
CONDITIONAL MOOD : ıoꝼꝼaınn.

With the usual terminations for the other persons and numbers.

1. The past indicative is either the regular form ḋ'ıċeap, &c., or the irregular ḋuap (with the usual terminations :—ḋuaıp, ḋuaıḋ pé, &c.)

2. The infinitive is ḋ'ıċe.

3. In other respects this verb is regular.

(12.) Rıɥım, *I reach.*

IMPERATIVE MOOD.

Singular.	Plural.
1. . . .	1. pıɥmíp.
2. pıɥ.	2. pıɥíḋ.
3. pıɥeaḋ pé.	3. pıɥıḋıp.

INDICATIVE MOOD.

Present Tense.

Singular.	Plural.
1. pıɥım	1. pıɥmíḋ.
2. pıɥıp	2. pıɥċí.
3. pıɥ pé.	3. pıɥıḋ.

Past.

1. pánȝap.
2. pánȝaip.
3. pámȝ ré, pánaiȝ ré.

1. pánȝaman.
2. pánȝabap.
3. pánȝabap.

First Person Singular.

Consuet Past : piȝinn.
Future : piȝfead.
Conditional piȝfinn.
Mood :

} With the usual terminations for the other persons and numbers.

Infinitive ; do piaċtain or do poċtain.

1. The past, future, and conditional, are sometimes expressed by a different verb, as follows :— but this form (which is the same form as the infinitive), is not often met with in the modern language.

First Person Singular.

Past : piaċtap.
Future : piaċtrad.
Conditional piaċtrainn.
Mood :

} With the usual terminations for the other persons and numbers.

(13.) Téidim, *I go.*

Imperative Mood.

Singular.
1. . . .
2. téid.
3. teidead ré.

Plural.
1. téidmír.
2. téidid.
3. téiddír.

Indicative Mood.

Present Tense.

Singular.
1. téidim.
2. téidir.
3. téid ré.

Plural.
1. téidmíd.
2. téidtid or téitid.
3. téidid.

CHAP. V.] THE VERB. 83

Past Tense.

1. ċuaḋar.
2. ċuaḋair.
3. ċuaiḋ ré.

1. ċuaḋmar.
2. ċuaḃḃar.
3. ċuaḋḋar.

There is another form of the past tense of this verb used after the particles ᵹo, ní, &c., which O'Donovan classes as a subjunctive mood. The negative ní, which aspirates, is here prefixed: after ᵹo, the initial would be eclipsed.

1. ní ḋeaċar.
2. ní ḋeaċair.
3. ní ḋeaċaiḋ ré.

1. ní ḋeaċamar.
2. ní ḋeaċaḃar.
3. ní ḋeaċaḋar.

	First Person Singular.	
Consuet Past :	ċéiḋimn.	⎫ With the usual terminations for the other persons and numbers.
Future :	paċpaḋ or paċaḋ.	
CONDITIONAL MOOD :	paċpainn or paċainn.	

INFINITIVE ; do ḋul.   PARTICIPLE ; aᵹ ḋul.

(14.) tiᵹim, *I come.*

IMPERATIVE MOOD.

Singular.
1. . . .
2. tar or tiᵹ.
3. tiᵹeaḋ ré.

Plural.
1. tiᵹimír or tiᵹeam.
2. tiᵹiḋ.
3. tiᵹiḋír.

INDICATIVE MOOD

Present Tense.

1. tiᵹim.
2. tiᵹir.
3. tiᵹ ré.

1. tiᵹimíḋ.
2. tiᵹiḋ, tiᵹṫiḋ.
3. tiᵹio.

84 ETYMOLOGY. [PART II.

Past Tense.

1. ċánġar.
2. ċánġair.
3. ċáinic ré.

1. ċánġamar.
2. ċánġabar.
3. ċánġadar.

First Person Singular

Consuet Past   ċiġinn.
Future: ciocfad.

Conditional Mood: ciocfainn

} With the usual terminations for the other persons and numbers.

Infinitive; do ċeaċt.   Participle; aġ ceaċt.

OTHER DEFECTIVE VERBS.

1. The following defective verbs are often met with in the modern language.

Cir or ar, "says." It is used only in the third person, much like the English defective verb *quoth;* as, air ré, says he: cread do déunrair dam? ar Diarmaid: "'What wilt thou do for me?' says Diarmaid;" déan eólur dúinn mar a b-ruil ré, ar riad, "'give knowledge to us where he is,' said they (or say they)." In the older writings this verb is often written ol.

At baċ, he (or she) died.

Dar, it seems, it seemed, or it might seem (according to the tense or mood of the verb with which it is connected). Dar liom, methinks or methought; dar leat it seems or seemed to thee; and so on with the rest of these prepositional pronouns singular and plural: Do riċ ré, dar liom, mar an ġaoiċ, he ran, methought (or it seemed to me) like the wind.

Oliġċear, it is lawful, it is allowed.

Ður, to know; ċainic ré ður an raiḃ riaḋ ann, he came (in order) to know whether they were there.

Feaḋar, I know; used only negatively and interrogatively, and in the present tense: ní ḟeaḋar mé, I do not know; ní ḟeaḋar ré, he does not know; an ḃ-ḟeaḋraḃar? do ye know?

Ní ḟuláir, it is necessary (or "must," used impersonally); ní ḟuláir ḋam a ḃeiṫ air riuḃal, "it is necessary for me to be (or I must be) walking (away)."

CHAPTER VI.
ADVERBS, PREPOSITIONS, CONJUNCTIONS, INTERJECTIONS.

I. ADVERBS.

1. There are not many simple adverbs in the Irish language. Far the greatest number of the Irish adverbs are compounds of two or more words.

2. An adverb may be formed from an adjective by prefixing the particle ɣo, which in this application has the same effect as the English postfix *ly;* as borḃ, fierce; ɣo borḃ, fiercely. Almost all Irish adjectives admit of being changed in this manner to adverbs.

3. Besides the adverbs formed in this way, there are many compound adverbs, which are generally made up of a noun and a preposition; the preposition often causing an eclipsis.

4. The following is an alphabetical list of the compound adverbs in most general use, with a few of the simple adverbs. Some of the compound adverbs become, in some situations, prepositions:—

A ḃ-faḋ, far off, in space or time.
Aḃur, on this side. (See ṫall.)
A ḋ-toraċ, at first, in the beginning.
A ḋ-tuaiḋ, northwards.
A ɣ-céaḋóir, immediately.

A g-céin, far off.
A g-coṁnuiḋe, always.
Aġ ṗin, there.
Aġ ṗo, here.
Aġ ṗúḋ, yonder.
Aiṗ aiṗ, back, backward. (See aiṗ éiġin.)
Aiṗ ball, on the spot, instantly.
Aiṗ biṫ, at all.
Aiṗ bun, on foundation: cuṗ aiṗ bun, to found, to institute.
Aiṗ ċeana, in like manner; in general.
Aiṗ ċoiḋċe, for ever.
Aiṗ éiġin, with difficulty; perforce:—aiṗ aiṗ no aiṗ éiġin, by consent or by force: *nolens volens; willy nilly.*
Aiṗ g-cúl, backwards, back: cuṗ aiṗ g-cúl—the opposite to cuṗ aiṗ bun—to put back, to abolish.
Aiṗ leiṫ, apart, separately.
Aiṗ ṁoḋ, in a manner; so that.
Aiṗ ṗon, for the sake of.
Aiṗ uaiṗiḃ, at times; sometimes.
Amaċ, out of, outside.
Aṁáin, alone, only.
Amáṗaċ, to-morrow.
Amuiġ, outside.
Aṁuil, like, as.
An áiṗḋe, on high.
Ané, yesterday.
Aníoṗ, from below, upwards.
Ann éinḟeaċṫ, together.
Ann ṗin, there.
Ann ṗo, here.
Ann ṗúḋ, yonder.
A nḋeaṗ, southward.
Anaiċe, near.

Anall, to this side; hither.
A ngaṗ, near.
Aniu, to-day.
Anoiṗ, now.
Anonn, to that side; thither.
An ṫan, when.
Anuaṗ, from above, downwards.
Apéiṗ, last night.
Aṗiaiṁ, ever.
Aṗíṗ, again.
Aṗṫeaċ, in, into.
Aṗṫiġ, in, inside.
Beaġ naċ, little but; almost.
Cá h-aṗ, caḋ aṗ, canaṗ, from what? whence?
Cá ṁéiḋ, how many? how much?
Cáiṫ, cá h-áiṫ, cia áiṫ, what place?
De ḃṗiġ, because.
Do ṗíoṗ, always.
Caḋon, that is; *i.e.; id est.*
Ḟá, gives an adverbial meaning to some words.
Ḟá ċéaḋóiṗ, immediately.
Ḟá ḋeoiġ, at last.
Ḟá ḋó, twice.
Ḟá ṗeaċ, by turns; respectively.
Ḟa ṫṗí, thrice.
Ġo bṗáṫ, for ever (lit. to [the] judgment).
Ġo ḋeiṁin, verily; truly; indeed.
Ġo ḋ-ṫí, unto.
Ġo ḟóil, yet; awhile.
Ġo h-iomlán, altogether.
Ġo léiṗ, entirely.
Ġo leóṗ, enough.
Iomoṗṗo, however, moreover, indeed.
Maille ṗe, together with.
Maṗ an g-céaḋna, likewise; in like manner.

CHAP. VI.] PREPOSITIONS. 87

Maṙ aon le, together with.
No ɼo, until.
O ṗoin ale, from that time out.
Oṗ cionn, above.
Síoṗ, downwards.
Soiṗ, eastwards.
Suaṗ, upwards.
Ṫall, on the other side; beyond. (See Áḃuṗ.)
Ṫamall, awhile.
Ṫuille eile, besides; moreover.

II. PREPOSITIONS.

1. The following is a list of the simple prepositions :—

Á or i, in ; as a mbaile, in the town.
Á, out of, or from (unusual); as a Muṁain, out of Munster.
Áɼ or aiɼ, at, with.
Áiṗ, aṗ, upon.
Ánn, in. This takes ṗ before the article. (See page 17.)
Áṗ, out of.
Chum, to or towards, for the purpose of.
Ḋaṗ, used in swearing, equivalent to *by:* ḋaṗ mo ḃṗiaṫaṗ, " by my word."
Ḋo, to. Ḋe, from, off, of.
Eaḋaṗ, the same as iḋiṗ.
Fá or faoi, under.
Ɉan, without.
Ɉo, towards, along with. It takes ṗ before the article an ; as ɼuṗ an ḋ-ṫiɼ, to the house.

I, the same as á.
Iaṗ, after. It takes ṗ before the article (an), and becomes iaṗṗ.
Iḋiṗ, between.
Im, the same as um.
Le or ṗe, with. It takes ṗ before the article (an), and then becomes leiṗ or ṗiṗ.
Maṗ, like, as.
O, from.
Oṗ, over, above.
Re, ṗia, before. It takes ṗ before the article (an).
Seaċ, beyond, besides.
Ṫaṗ, over, across. It takes ṗ before the article (an), and then becomes ṫaṗṗ.
Ṫṗé, through. It takes ṗ before the article, and then becomes ṫṗéṗ.
Ṫṗíḋ, the same as ṫṗé.
Um or im, about.

2. Some of the simple prepositions are amalgamated with the personal and possessive pronouns, for which see pages 41, 45.

3. Besides the simple prepositions, there are in Irish a number of compound prepositions. Each of these consists of a simple preposition followed by a noun; and in many of them the initial of the noun is eclipsed by the influence of the simple preposition. In some cases the preposition has dropped out and only the noun remains.

4. The following is a list of the most usual compound prepositions, with their meanings:—

A b-ṗiaḋnaiṙe, in presence of.
A b-ṗoċaiṙ, with, along with.
A b-ṫaoib, in regard to, concerning.
A b-ṫiṁċeall: see ṫiṁċeall,
A ʒ-ceann, at the head of, at the end of, with regard to.
A ʒ-coinne, against, for (in the phrase to go *for*): ṗiċiḋ a ʒ-coinne a ċéile, "they run against each other:" do ċuaiḋ ṙe a ʒ-coinne a aṫaṙ, he went for his father.
A ʒ-coiṙ, by the side of, hard by, along. This is often contracted to coiṙ: coiṙ na bṙíġḋe, "beside the (river) Bride."
A h-aiċle, after: a h-aiċle na laoiḋe ṙin, "after that lay."
Ameaṙʒ, amongst: ṙíoṙ ameaṙʒ na ʒ-coillṫeaḋ, "down amongst the woods."
A láṫaiṙ, in presence of.
Aiṙ aġaiḋ, forward, over against, opposite: dul aiṙ aġaiḋ, to go forward, to progress: aiṙ aġaiḋ na ʒaoiṫe, opposite (exposed to) the wind.
Aiṙ béalaiḋ, in front of, opposite: do luiġḋíṙ do ġnáṫ a n-ioṁḋaiḋ aṙ béalaiḋ a n-aṫaṙ, "they used to lie, customarily, in beds opposite their father" (Children of Lir).
Aiṙ bun, on foundation.
Aiṙ ċeann, for (in the phrase to go for); as a duḋaiṙṫ Naiṙe le h-Aṙḋán dul aiṙ ċenn Ḟeṙʒuiṙ, "Naisi said to Ardan to go for Fergus."
Aiṙ ḟeaḋ, through, throughout, during: aiṙ ḟeaḋ bliaḋna, "during a year."
Aiṙ ḟuḋ, thoughout, amongst aiṙ ḟuḋ na d-tonn, amongst the waves.
Aiṙ ʒ-cúl, behind.
Aiṙ ṙon, for the sake of, although.
A n-ḋiaiḋ, after: a n-ḋiaiḋ a ċéile, after one another, one after another.
Coiṙ, contracted from a ʒ-coiṙ.
Ḋála, as to: ḋála Blánaiḋe, "as to Blanaid."
D'éiṙ, after: d'éiṙ na díliṅṅe, "after the deluge."
D'ionnṙaiġiḋ or d'ionnṙaiġe, towards: ʒluaiṙeaṙ ṙóiṁe d'ionnṙaiġe a luinʒe, "he goes forward towards his ship."

Dočum, towards.
Do ṗéip, according to.
Ꝃo nuiɼe, unto, until.
Ꝃo ḃ-ɕí, to, unto, as far as: ꞅiuḃail ɼo ḃ-ɕí an ḋoꞃuꞅ, walk to the door.
Iomċúꞃa, as to: iomċúꞃa Ꝑhinn, "as to Finn."
Ꝑá ċuaiꞃim, towards.
Láiṁ le or láiṁ ꞃe, near, by, beside: ꞅuiḋ láiṁ liom, sit near me; láiṁ ꞃe beannaiḃ boiꞃċe, "beside Beanna Boirche."
Oꞃ cionn, over, above: Ꝃꞃaḋuiɼ Dia óꞃ cionn ɼaċ uile niḋ, "love God above all things:" ꞃo éiꞃiɼ oꞃ cionn an ɼaoi, "he rose over the spear."
I ɼ-cionn, the same as a ɼ-ceann: i ɼ-cionn na bliaḋna, "at the end of the year."
Ꞇaꞃ ċeann, besides, for the sake of, beyond, in preference to.
Ꞇaꞃ aiꞃ, backwards; same as aiꞃ aiꞃ.
Ꞇaꞃ éiꞅ, after; the same as ḋéiꞅ: ɕaꞃ éiꞅ na Saṁna, " after the Samhain (1st of November)."
Ꞇimċeall, about, around: ɕeaċɕ ɕimċeall Ḋhiaꞃmaḋa, "to go around Dermat."
Oꞃ coṁaiꞃ, in presence of, before the face of: óꞃ coṁaiꞃ Ꝑhinn, "in presence of Finn."

III. CONJUNCTIONS.

1. There are few simple conjunctions in the Irish language.

2. There are, however, many compound conjunctions, much like the English conjunctional phrases, "for the reason that," "to the end that," &c.

3. Generally speaking, the meanings of the compound conjunctions may be easily gathered from the signification of the words that compose them; but there are a few whose meanings are not so plain.

4. The following is a list of the simple conjunctions with their meanings, together with those of the compound conjunctions whose meanin are not quite obvious.

Acṫ, but, except.
Acṫ ċeana, but however.
Aġuṗ, and; often contracted to a'ṗ, aṗ, and 'ṗ.
Aiṗ an aḃḃaṗ ṗin, wherefore.
An, an interrogative particle: an ḃ-ḟuil ṗí ṗlán? Is she well?
Aṗ, the same as the last, only used with the past tense. See p. 58.
bíoḋ, although: it is really the third singular imperative of the verb táim.
Cíḋ: see ġíḋ.
Cóiṁ, as.
Dá, if: sometimes written ḋá mo.
Do ḃṗiġ, because.
Do ċum ġo, in order that.
Fóṗ, yet, moreover.
Ġiḋ or ġiḋeaḋ, although.
Ġo, that.
Ġonaḋ aiṗe ṗin, wherefore.

Ġuṗ, that: formed of the preceding and ṗo: see p. 58.
Ioná, iná: see ná.
Ionnuṗ ġo, in order that, so that.
Má, if.
Má tá ġo, although that.
Maṗ, as: see muna.
Muna, if not, unless; often written muṗ, and even (corruptly) maṗ.
Maiṗeaḋ, if so, well then.
Maṗ ṗin, maṗ ṗo, in that manner, in this manner: thus.
Ná, than: see ioná.
Ná, nor, not.
Nó, or: often pronounced nú in Munster.
O, since, seeing that, because.
O ċáṗla, since, whereas.
Oiṗ, because.
Sul, before.
Uime ṗin, therefore, wherefore.

IV. INTERJECTIONS.

1. The following is a list of the most common interjections. Besides these there are many interjectional expressions somewhat like the English, "O shame!" "Alack! and well-a-day!" but it is not necessary to enumerate them:—

A, the sign of the vocative case, usually translated O.
Aṗ tṗuaġ, alas! what pity!
Eiṗt, hush! list!
Faṗaoṗ, faṗaoiṗ, alas!
Faṗaoiṗ ġeuṗ, alas! O sharp sorrow!
Féaċ, see! behold!
Maiṗġ, woe! O sad!

Monáiṗe, O shame!
Monuaṗ, alas! woe is me!
Mo ṫṗuaġ: see aṗ tṗuaġ.
Oċ, uċ, alas!
Oċón, or uċón, alas! written oċán or uċán in old writings.
Olaġón, alas!

CHAPTER VII.

PREFIXES AND AFFIXES.

1. There are in Irish, as in other languages, prefixes and affixes, which modify the meanings of words.

I. PREFIXES.

1. The following is a list of the principal prefixes with their meanings: it will be observed that many of them have a double form, which arises from conformity to the rule caol le caol &c.

2. Most of these are inseparable particles; but a few are also employed independently as separate words.

ᴀɪʀ or eɪʀ, back or again, like English *re:* as ıoc, payment; aıʀıoc, repayment, restitution: eıʀġe, rising; eıʀeıʀġe resurrection.

Aṁ or aɪṁ, a negative particle, like English *un:* as péıḋ, open, clear; aıṁṗéıḋ, difficult, rough.

An, an intensive particle: as luatġáıʀeaċ, joyful; as an-luatġáıʀeaċ, overjoyed.

An or aın, a negative particle, like English *un:* as tʀát time; antʀát, untimely: mían, desire; aınṁıan, evil desire.

At, a reiterative, like English *re:* as ʀáḋ, a saying; atʀáḋ a repetition.

At has sometimes the meaning of English *dis* in *dismantle*: as cuma, a form; atċumaḋ, to deform, to destroy; ʀıoġaḋ, to crown or elect a king; aıtʀıoġaḋ, to dethrone.

ban, feminine (from bean, a woman); as eaċlaċ, a messenger; ban-eaċlaċ or baın-eaċlaċ, a female messenger.

bıt or bıot, lasting, constant: as beó, living; bıtḃeó, everlasting.

Cóṁ, equal : English *co* or *con :* as aimpeap, time ; cóṁ-aimpeapaċ, contemporary.

Deaġ, deiġ, good : as blap, taste ; deaġḃlap, good or pleasant taste.

Dí, dío, a negative, like English *dis :* as céilliḋe, wise ; dí-céilliḋe, foolish : ceann, a head ; díċeannaḋ, to behead.

Dpoċ, dpoiċ, bad or evil : as obaip, a work ; dpoċ-obaip an evil work.

Do and po are opposites, as are also often the letters d and p. Do denotes difficulty, or ill, or the absence of some good or positive quality : as paicpeanaċ or popaicpeanaċ, visible ; do-paicpeanaċ, invisible : doláp, tribulation ; póláp, comfort : donap, ill luck ; ponap, good luck : do-ḋéunta, hard to be done ; po-ḋéunta, easy to be done : dubaċ, sad ; pubaċ, merry.

Ea, a negative, often causing eclipsis : as daingean, strong ; éadaingean, weak : cóip, just ; éaġcóip, injustice : tpom, heavy ; éadtpom, light.

Eap, a negative : as onóip, honour ; eapónóip, dishonour : plán, healthful ; eaplán, sick : caipdeap, friendship ; eap-caipdeap, enmity.

Fo, under : as duine, a man ; foḋuine, an *under-man*, a common man, a servant.

Fpiṫ, against, back, *contra :* as buille, a stroke ; fpiṫbuille, a back stroke : bac, a hook ; fpiotbac, a *back-hook*, a barb.

Il, iol, many : as iomaḋ, much ; iliomaḋ, sundry, various : daṫ, a colour ; ioldaṫaċ, many coloured : paoḃap, an edge ; iolpaoḃaip, many-edged weapons.

In, ion, fit : as déunta, done ; indéunta, fit to be done : paiḋte, said ; ionpaiḋte, fit to be said.

Lán, full, used as an intensive : as aiḃḃéil, vast ; lánaiḃ-ḃéil, awfully vast.

Leaṫ, half : as uaip, an hour ; leaṫuaip, half an hour. This word is also used to denote one of a pair : thus púil, an eye ; leaṫ-púil (literally *half an eye*), one of two eyes. See "Idiom, No. 13."

Mí, mío, a negative : as meap, respect ; míṁeap, disrespect : cóṁaiple, advice ; miocóṁaiple, evil advice.

Neaṁ, neiṁ, a negative : as coimpiġte, comprehensible ; neaṁcoimpiġte, incomprehensible : niḋ, a thing ; neiṁniḋ, nothing.

Reuṁ, before, like English *pre :* as paiḋte, said ; peuṁ paiḋte, aforesaid.

Ro, an intensive particle : as móp, great ; pó-ṁóp, very great.

CHAP. VII.] PREFIXES AND AFFIXES. 93

Sár, an intensitive particle: as maiṫ, good; ráp-ṁaiṫ, very good.

So, ſoı, the opposite to do, denotes apt, easy, good as ḃeaṗḃṫa, proved; ſoıḃeaṗḃṫa, easily proved.

Uṗ or úıṗ, an intensitive particle: as íſeal, low; úıṗíſeal, very low, humble, mean, vile.

II. AFFIXES OR TERMINATIONS.*

1. The following is a list of the principal affixes or terminations, with their meanings; but it does not include inflectional terminations, which are all given in connection with declensions and conjugations.

Aċ, when it is the termination of an adjective, means full of, abounding in, like the English *y* and *ous*, with the former of which it seems cognate; as ḃṗaıǵean, the black-thorn; ḃṗaıǵeanaċ, abounding in black-thorn: ḃṗiaṫaṗ, a word; ḃṗiaṫṗaċ, wordy, talkative.

Aċ, as the termination of a noun, generally denotes a personal agent; as cúṁaċḋ, power: cúṁaċḋaċ, a mighty person: Connaċtaċ, a native of Connaught.

Aċt, an abstract termination, like the English *ness* and *ty* (in *probity*): as caṗtanaċ, charitable: caṗtanaċt, charity: móṗ and móṗḋa, great; moṗḋaċt, greatness.

Aıḋe, uıḋe, or ıḋe, a personal termination, denoting a doer; as coṗ, a foot; coıṗıḋe, a walker: ṫıoman, drive; ṫıomanaıḋe, a driver.

Aıṗe or ıṗe, a personal termination, denoting an agent or doer; as loṗǵ, a track; loṗǵaıṗe, a tracker: cealǵ, guile; cealǵaıṗe, a deceiver.

Aṁaıl has the same meaning as the English *like* and *ly*: as ṗlaıṫ, a prince; ṗlaıṫeaṁaıl, princely.

An, a diminutive termination, but it has now nearly lost its diminutive sense; as loċ a lake; loċán, a small lake.

Aṗ or eaṗ, and sometimes the letter ṗ alone, a termination denoting abstract quality, like aċt; as aoıḃınn, delightful;

---

* For a full account of these terminations see the author's "Origin and History of Irish Names of Places." Second series, Chaps. I. and II.

aoıbneaṗ, delightfulness or delight: ceann, a head; ceannaṗ, headship, authority.

Ḃhaṅ and ḃne have a collective or cumulative sense; as ḃuılle, a leaf; ḃuılleaḃaṅ, foliage: ḋaıṗ, an oak; ḋaıṗḃṅe, a place of oaks.

Cḣaṅ has a collective sense like the last; as ḃeann, a peak or gable; beannċaṅ, abounding in peaks or gables.

Ḋe, an ancient adjectival termination, has much the same meaning as the English *ful* and *ly* (in manly). In the modern language it is varied to the forms ḋa, ṫa, and ṫa; as móṅ, great; móṗḋa, majestic: ṗeaṗ, a man; ṗeaṅḋa, manly: míle, a champion; míleaḋṫa, champion-like, knightly.

Ċ denotes abstract quality, like aċṫ; as ṗınn, fair or white; ṗınne, fairness: ḃoġ, soft; ḃuıġe, softness.

Ín, a diminutive termination. This may be said to be the only diminutive that still retains its full force in the living language; and it is much used in Ireland even where Irish is not spoken. bóṫaṅ, a road; bóṫaıṗín (*bohereen*), a little road: *crusk*, a pitcher; *cruiskeen*, a little pitcher.

Laċ, naċ, ṗaċ, ṫaċ, ṫṅaċ, have all the same meaning as aċ, namely, full of, abounding in; as bṅıṗ, break; bṅıṗleaċ, a breach, a complete defeat: muc, a pig; muclaċ, a piggery: luaċaıṗ, rushes; luaċaṗnaċ, a rushy place: boġ, a bog or soft place; boġṅaċ, a place full of bogs: coıll, a wood; coılltéaċ, a woody place. These seem to be cognate with the terminations in the English words *poult-ry*, *varie-ty*, &c.

Ṁlhaṅ means abounding in, like the English *ful* and *ly*; as bṅıġ, power; bṅıoġṁaṅ, powerful.

Oġ, a diminutive termination; as cíaṅ, black; cíaṅoġ, a black little animal (a clock): ġaḃal, a fork; ġaḃalóġ, a little fork.

Oıṗ, or ḋóıṗ, or ṫóıṗ, denotes an agent or doer, the same as the English *er* in *reaper;* as buaıl, strike; buaılṫeóıṗ, thresher: coınneal, a candle; coınnleóıṗ, a candlestick ṗeal, a scythe; ṗealaḋóıṗ, a mower.

Re has a collective signification, like ḃaṅ; as beul, the mouth; bélṅe, language, speech.

Seaċ is used as a sort of feminine termination; as ġall, an Englishman; ġaıllṗeaċ, an Englishwoman: óıṅeaċ, a female fool (from an old root ón, whence the old word ón mıṫ, a fool, the equivalent of the modern amaḋán).

Ṫaċ and ṫṅaċ: see laċ.

PART III.
SYNTAX.*

CHAPTER I.
NOUNS.

1. When two nouns come together signifying different things, the second one is in the genitive case; as ⁊ᴜᴄ ᵹaᴅaɪꝑ, the voice of a hound; ɪ ʙ-ꝑlaɪᴄɪoꝑ Єꝑeann, "in the sovereignty of Erin;" báꝑꝑ na h-ɪnꝑe, the top of the island.

The noun in the genitive always follows the noun that governs it.

2. When the genitive noun is singular masculine, its initial is aspirated if the article is used; as mac an ꝑɪꝑ, the son of the man. (See pages 17, 18, for this rule and its exceptions).

3. When the article is not used with the governed noun in the singular number, the initial of the latter is generally not aspirated (except in the case mentioned in next Rule); as Conall ɪ ᵹ-cꝑoᴄaɪʙ báɪꝑ, "Conall in the forms *of death;*" a n-ᴅólá[ꝑ bꝑóɪᴅe a'ꝑ péɪne, "in the sorrow *of bondage* and *of pain.*"

---

* Several of the rules of Syntax have been unavoidably anticipated in Orthography and Etymology, as they are in every Irish Grammar. These rules will be referred to in their proper places in this Syntax, or repeated when thought necessary.

4. When the noun in the genitive is a proper name, its initial is generally aspirated, even though the article is not used; as ρlıoċτ Ṡhaoιδıl, "the race of Gaodhal;" cloıδeaṁ Mhanannaın, "the sword of Manannan."

Exception:—In this case, ϼ and τ often resist aspiration (p. 34); as Cιρe ιnġean Ꝺealḃaoιċ, "Eirè, the daughter of Dealbhaoth."

5. If the governed noun be in the genitive plural, its initial is eclipsed with the article, (for which see page 18); and the initial is generally aspirated, if the article is not used; as Ꝺaιnġen ṁac n-Uιρneaċ, "the fortress *of* [*the*] *sons* of Usna;" buιδean ċuρaδ, "a company of knights;" δıaρ ḃan, "two women" (or rather "a pair of women").

Even in the absence of the article however, an eclipsis sometimes occurs; as naoı naonḃaρ δo ḃí aʒ τeaċτ δ'ıaρραιδ cíoρa aʒuρ cána ḃ-ρeaρ n-Cιριonn, "nine times nine persons who were coming to demand the taxes and tributes *of the men* of Erin."

Sometimes also, in the absence of the article, the noun in the genitive plural is neither aspirated nor eclipsed.

6. When two nouns come together signifying the same thing (or in apposition), they generally agree in case; as Nuaδa Ⲁιρʒıoḃláṁ mac Eaċτaιġ mıc Eaδaρlaṁ, "Nuadha Silver-hand, son of Eachtach, son of Eadarlamh;" na δ-τρí ḃ-Ƒιnneaṁna, mac Eoċaıδ, "of the three Finnavnas, sons of Eochad."

Here, in the first example, Nuaδa is nominative, and so is mac, which is in apposition to it; Eaċτaıġ is genitive, and so is the next word, mıc, which is in apposition to it. In the second example, Ƒιnneaṁna is in the genitive (plural), and mac also, in opposition to it, is in the genitive (plural).

For exceptions to this Rule, see "Idioms," No. 33, p. 129. See also next rule.

7. The last rule is not always observed: departures from it are sometimes found, even in good Irish writings; as, ρáιnnıδe buıδe óρδa maρ bióeaó aṗ Mháiṗe, bean Sheaġain an ṗíġeaḋóṗa, "yellow gold rings as used-to-be on Mary, wife of John (the son of) the weaver;" ċainic ṗiġ Chiaṗ-ṗuiḋe Luaċṗa ḋ'ṗioṗ a ċoṁḋalta, eaḋon, Cian mac Oiliolla, "the King of Kerry-Luachra came to visit his foster-son, that is, Cian, the son of Oilioll: ḋo ṫṗiall (Oṗcaṗ) a ġ-coinne Mheaṗġaiġ ṁiṗe, an tṗéan leoṁan "Oscar went to meet the furious Meargach, *the strong lion*."

The first example exhibits a disagreement in case between Mháiṗe and bean, which are in apposition, the former being dative (after aṗ), the latter nominative (its dative would be mnaoi, p. 29). In the second example ċoṁḋalta is genitive (after the infinitive, Rule 15, p. 112), and Cian, in apposition to it, is nominative (its genitive would be Céin). In the last example Mheaṗġaiġ is genitive, and leoṁan, in apposition to it, is nominative. This last example however, seems properly to belong to a class of exceptions to Rule 7 which are explained further on ("Idioms:" No. 33, page 129).

8. A noun used adjectively in English is commonly expressed in Irish by a genitive case; as English, "a gold ring," Irish, ṗáinne óiṗ, a ring of gold. This form of expression is very common in Irish; as ṗeaṗ ḋliġe, a lawyer; literally "a man of law."

9. Collective nouns are singular in form, and as such they take the singular form of the article (when the article is used); but they are plural in signification, and as such they generally take adjectives and pronouns in the plural number, and also verbs in the plural, when, in accordance with Par. 9, p. 50, the plural form of the verb is used; as, noċtuiḋ an ṗuiṗeann ṗin, "that company disclose;" tanġaḋaṗ an buiḋean ċuṗaḋ ṗin ḋo láṫaiṗ Ṗhinn, aġuṗ ḋo ḃeannuiġ ṗiaḋ ḋo, "that *company* of knights *came* to the presence of Finn, and *they* saluted him."

The personal nouns from biaṗ to ḋeiċneaḃaṗ, mentioned at page 39, follow this rule: as ḋo ḃaḋaṗ an biaṗ ṗin ġo h-imṗeaṗnaċ, "that pair were at strife."

10. Nouns denoting a part commonly take ᴅe with the dative of the nouns (or pronouns) of which they form a part; as ʒaᴅap ᴅ'áp nʒaᴅapaıᴅ, "a hound of our hounds;" aon caop ᴅıoᴅ, "one berry of them;" ʒac ᴅuıne ᴅe'n pobul, "each person of the people."

11. The personal nouns from ᴅıap to ᴅeıcneaᴅap inclusive (p. 39,) and also ceópa, three, generally govern nouns in the genitive plural; as ᴅıap ᴅan, "two (of) women;" a cpıúp mac aʒup a ᴅ-cpıup ᴅan, "his three sons and their three wives;" ceópa ᴅan, "three women;" naonᴅap caoıpeac, "nine chieftains."

But they sometimes take ᴅe with the dative as in last rule; as naoı naonᴅap ᴅo maopaıᴅ na ᴅ-ᴘómopac, "nine times nine *of the stewards* of the Fomorians:" mo ᴅíp mac, mo ᴅíp ᴅ'ᴘeapaıᴅ, "my two sons, my two men."

CHAPTER II.

THE ARTICLE AND NOUN.

1. The article agrees with its noun in number, gender, and case; as an ᴘeap, the man; na cıpce, of the hen; na ba, the cows.

2. For the influence of the article on the noun, see p. 17.

3. When one noun governs another in the genitive, the article can be used only with the latter. Thus, in English we can say "the age of the world" (using the definite article with each noun); but in Irish, the corresponding expression is, aoıp an ᴅomaın, not, an aoıp an ᴅomaın.

Exception:—When a demonstrative pronoun follows the governing noun, or when the two nouns come together as a compound word, the governing noun may take the article; as an c-oıᴅe múınce, the teacher; má ᴅo ᴅeıp cú an áıpeaᴅ pın ᴅúınn 'pan ló po na n-ᴅeóp, "if thou givest so much to us in this day of tears." Here the article is used before both ló and ɒeóρ. Canɡaɒan aηíρ ı n-Eιρınn an ρlιoċc ρo Shimeon bhριc, " these descendants of Simon Brec came again into Erin:" here the article is used before ρlιoċc, the governing noun.

4. When a possessive pronoun is used with the genitive noun, the article cannot be used with either; thus, "the house of my father" is ceaċ m'acaρ, not an ceaċ m'acaρ.

The peculiarity noticed in the last two rules exists also in English when the possessive case is used, i.e., the article can be used only with the possessive noun, as the world's age; my father's house.

5. When a demonstrative pronoun is used with a noun, the article is also used; as an ρean ριn, that man, literally "the man that;" na mná úɒ, yonder women : literally "the women yonder."

6. The article is used before the names of some countries and cities, where the definite article would not be used in English ; as Moenan, abb Cacρaċ Puρρa ιρın Pρaınc, ɒéuʒ, "Moenan, abbot of Caher Fursa, in (the) France, died;" Cρuaċa na h-Eιρeann, "the stacks of (the) Erin;" cuaιρceaρc na h-Aρıa, "the north of (the) Asia." There is in Irish also a form of phrase corresponding to the English "the mighty Hector;" as an c-Oρcaρ áʒ, "the noble Oscar."

7. When an adjective is predicated of a noun by the verb ιρ (in any of its forms), the article is used with the noun (but in the corresponding expression in English the definite article would not be used); as ιρ maιċ an ρean é, he is a good man : literally "he is the good man."

9. The Irish article is used before abstract nouns much more commonly than the English definite article; as an c-ocρuρ, the hunger; cρí nιɒ ɒo cím:—an peacaɒ, an báρ, a'ρ an ρían, "three things I see, *the* sin, *the* death, and *the* pain."

CHAPTER III.

THE ADJECTIVE AND NOUN.

1. Adjectives denoting fulness or a part of anything may take either the dative after ᴅe or the genitive; as (dative after ᴅe):—ıᴅıꞃ ᴅá ᴅaꞃaıle lán ᴅe leann, "between two barrels full of ale;" ᴅá mé lán ᴅo náıꞃe, "I am full of shame;" móꞃán ᴅ'uaıꞃlıᴅ, "many of nobles:" (genitive):—lán a ᴅuıꞃn, "the full of his fist;" an ꞃaıᴅ móꞃán aıꞃꞅıᴅ aıꞅe, "had he much *of money?*" cꞃaoᴅ ᴅꞃaoıꞅın aꞅuꞃ a lán áıꞃneaᴅ uıꞃꞃe, "a branch of blackthorn and its full *of sloes* on it."

2. The adjective in the comparative degree takes ná (or ıná or ıoná) before the noun which follows it; as ıꞅ ᴅınne a ceól ná lon 'ꞃná ꞃmól, "sweeter is her voice (music) than the blackbird and than the thrush."

Exception:—If the adjective in the comparative degree has ᴅe (" of it ") after it (see Idiom 39, p. 132), then ná is not used; as naċ ᴅu ꞃeıꞃꞃᴅe ᴅóıᴅ é, "that they would be none the better of it."

AGREEMENT AND COLLOCATION OF THE ADJECTIVE AND NOUN.

First Case: When the adjective is joined immediately with the noun.

> When the adjective is joined immediately with the noun as a qualifying or limiting term (as in the English "a high tower"), in this case the following **ten** rules apply.

1. The natural position of the adjective is after its noun; as caᴅlaċ móꞃ, "a great fleet."

The chief exceptions to this are stated in the next two rules.

2. Monosyllabic adjectives are often placed before their nouns; as caol-ḟear, "slender man;" mór ḟairrge, "great sea;" dub-ċarraig, "black rock."

3 This is especially the case with the following adjectives, some of which are hardly ever used after their nouns: deaġ, good; droċ, evil; ḟíor, true; nuaḋ, new; rean, old; tuaṫ, left-handed.

Numeral adjectives form another exception, for which see next chapter.

4. When a name consists of two words, the adjective comes between them; as Sliaḃ aḋḃal-mór Luaċra, "the tremendous-large Slieve Lougher;" Eaṁuin ṁín áluinn Maċa, "the smooth beautiful Eman Macha."

5. When the adjective follows its noun, it agrees with it in gender, number, and case; as ḟear maiṫ, a good man; rġéul na mná móire, "the story of the large woman" (gen. sing. fem.); ar an aiḋḃéir ionġantaiġ, "on the wonderful abyss" (dat. sing. fem.).

6. When the adjective follows its noun, the initial of the adjective is aspirated under the circumstances already stated in Par. 6, page 10; or eclipsed in the circumstance stated in Par. 3, page 34.

7. When two or more nouns are joined together, and are followed by an adjective which qualifies or limits them, all and each, the adjective agrees with the last: in other words, it is the last noun only that influences the adjective both in grammatical inflection, and in initial change; as bean aġur ḟear maiṫ, a good woman and man; ḟear aġur bean ṁaiṫ, a good man and woman.

8. When the adjective precedes the noun, as in Rules 2 and 3, above, it does not agree with the noun, i.e., it is not influenced by the noun,

either as to inflection, or as to initial change; in other words, the simple form of the adjective is used, whatever be the number, gender, or case of the noun; as mór uaiṗle, "great nobles;" do ṁór uaiṗliḃ, "to [the] great nobles;" bán cnoic Eireann, "the fair hills of Erin;" luaṫ barca, swift barks; fíor rgcul, "a true story;" fíor rgculta, "true stories."

9. When the adjective precedes the noun, the adjective and the noun are sometimes regarded as one compound word; and the initial of the noun is aspirated (in accordance with Par. 4, page 10): also the vowel of the adjective is often modified by the rule caol le caol &c.; as Deirḋre an Duiḃ-ṡleiḃe, "Deirdre of Dubh-Shliabh;" óig-ḃean, a young woman.

10. When the adjective precedes the noun, the initial of the adjective is subject to the same changes as if the adjective and the noun formed one word, i.e., one noun; as gáire na n-óig-ḟear, "the laughter of the young men;" an t-árd-ollaṁ rin, "that chief professor;" an t-rean-ḃean ḃoṫt, "the poor old woman."

SECOND CASE: When the adjective is connected with the noun by a verb.

When the adjective, instead of being joined immediately with the noun, is predicated of, or ascribed to, the noun by a verb of any kind (as in the English, "the man is tall," "he considered the man tall," "he made the knife sharp," "the roads were made straight"), in this case, the following **three** rules apply.

1. When an adjective is predicated of a noun by the verb tá, it follows the noun, the order being:—verb, noun, adjective; as tá an lá breáġ, the day is fine.

2. When an adjective is predicated of a noun

by the verb ıſ, it precedes the noun, the order being:—verb, adjective, noun; as ıſ bɾeáʒ an lá é, it is a fine day.

3. When an adjective is ascribed to a noun by a verb of any kind, the adjective does not agree with the noun, i.e., the adjective is not influenced by it, either initially or inflectionally; in other words, the simple form of the adjective, without inflection, is used, whatever be the number or gender of the noun; and the initial of the adjective is neither aspirated nor eclipsed (unless under the influence of some other word), as ıſ aıbınn ɖo cuaın acaɾ ɖo calaþuıɾc acaɾ ɖo ṁaʒa mínɾcocaca caeṁáılne, "delightful are thy harbours, and thy bays, and thy flowery lovely plains:" aʒuɾ cɾoıcne péıceaɓ aɾ na n-ɖacúʒaɓ ɖeaɾʒ, "and rams' skins dyed red."—(Exodus, xxv. 5).

The first example (from the story of the Children of Usna), exhibits both an agreement according to Rule 5, page 101, and a disagreement according to the present rule. For the three nouns are plural, and the two last adjectives which qualify them directly are in the plural form, while the first adjective aıbınn (modern aoıbınn) which is asserted of them by ıſ, is in its simple form (the plural would be aıbınne or aıbne). In the second example cɾoıcne is plural, while ɖeaɾʒ is singular (plural ɖeaɾʒa).

Observe the difference in meaning in the following, according to agreement or disagreement:—Ɖo ɾıʒne ɾé na bɾaıc ʒlaɾa; ɖo ɾıʒne ɾé na bɾaıc ʒlaɾ: in the first the adjective agrees with the noun, (both being plural), showing that it qualifies it directly (Rule 5, p. 101) and that the meaning is, "he made the green mantles;" in the second there is no agreement, (the adjective being singular and the noun plural), showing that the adjective is connected with the noun by the verb (Rule 3 above), and that the meaning is, "he made the mantles green."

CHAPTER IV.

NUMERAL ADJECTIVES.

1. A numeral adjective, whether cardinal or ordinal, when it consists of one word, goes before its noun; as τρί ρıρ, three men; ραn ϧαρα h-ἀιτ, "in the second place."

2. Numeral adjectives, both cardinal and ordinal, from 11 to 19 inclusive, take their nouns between the simple numeral and ϧέαʒ; as τρί capaill ϧέαʒ, thirteen horses; αn τρεαρ capall ϧέαʒ, the thirteenth horse.

3. Αοn, one; ϧά, two; céaϧ, first; and τρεαρ, third, cause aspiration; as αοn ḟεαρ, one man; ϧά ṁnαοι, two women; αṅ τρεαρ ḟεαċτ, "the third occasion."

4. The numerals ρεαċτ, οċτ, nαοι, and ϧειċ, cause eclipsis (except the noun begins with ρ, in which case there is no change), as ρεαċτ m-bliαϧnα, "seven years;" οċτ m-bα, "eight cows;" nαοι n-αιḃne, "nine rivers;" ϧειċ ḃ-ρıρ, "ten men."

5. The numerals τρί, ceıτρe, cúıʒ, ρέ, the ordinals (except céaϧ and τρεαρ: Rule 3 above), and the multiples of ten, cause no initial change; as ceıτρe ʒαϧαıρ, "four hounds."

6. Αοn, one, and all the multiples of ten, take their nouns in the singular number; as αοn lά, one day; céaϧ ceαnn, a hundred heads (lit. "a hundred head," just as we say "a hundred head of cattle"); τρί cαοʒαϧ laοċ, "three times fifty heroes;" míle bean, "a thousand women."

7. Dá, two, takes both the article and the noun in the singular number; and if the noun be feminine, it will be in the dative form; as ḋá ḟear, two men; an ḋá láiṁ, the two hands. (See next two rules).

8. If the noun following ḋá be in the genitive, it will be in the genitive plural; as lán a ḋá láṁ, "the full of his two hands."

9. Although ḋá takes the article and noun in the singular, yet the adjectives and pronouns referring to the noun will be in the plural, and the noun may also take a plural verb; as do ġluaiṗeaḋaṗ an ḋá ċṗéiṁṁíleaḋ ṗin, "these two strong heroes went;" ṗo ġaḃ a ḋá ṗleaġ ċṗó-ḟaiṗṗinġe ċṗann-ṗeaiṁṗa aṗ na ḃ-ṗoċṗuġaḋ a ḃ-ṗuil naċṗaċ neiṁe, "he took his two wide-socketed thick-handled spears, *they* having been bathed in the blood of serpents." Here the two adjectives and the pronoun referring to ṗleaġ, are plural.

CHAPTER V.

THE PRONOUN.

I. PERSONAL PRONOUNS.

1. Personal pronouns agree with the nouns they represent, in gender, number, and person; as iṗ maiṫ an ḃean í, she is a good woman; iṗ maiṫ an ḟeaṗ é, he is a good man; iṗ móṗ na ḋaoine iaḋ, they are great men.

2. A personal pronoun, or a possessive pronoun, which stands for a sentence or part of a sentence, is third person singular masculine; as ᴅá m-bϲɪᴅíp pɪp Cɪpeann an ᴜap n·aḋaɪᴅ, naċ ᴜu peɪppᴅe ᴅóɪᴜ é, "if the men of Erin were against you, they would not be the better of *it*;" (here the pronoun é stands for the sentence).

3. The accusative forms of the personal pronouns are often used as nominatives: always with ɪp (see Rule 18, p. 113), and with passive verbs (see Rule 20, p. 113); and sometimes with other verbs; as máp maɪċ na leaḋa pɪᴜ, ap éɪpíon, "'if ye are the good physicians,' says *he*."

II. POSSESSIVE PRONOUNS.

1. A possessive pronoun is never used without a noun.

In English there are distinct forms of the possessive pronouns which can stand without nouns (mine, thine, hers, &c.), but there are no forms corresponding to these in Irish.

2. The possessive pronouns precede their nouns; as mo máċaɪp, my mother; a ɢ-capbaᴅ, their chariot.

3. The possessives mo, my; ᴅo, thy; and a, his; aspirate the initials of their nouns; as mo ċeann, my head; ᴅo ċop, thy foot; a ṁeup, his finger.

4. The possessive a, her, requires the initial of its noun in its primitive state (neither aspirated nor eclipsed), and if the initial be a vowel, it prefixes h; as a máċaɪp, her mother; a h-aċaɪp, her father.

5. The possessives áp, our; ᴜap, your; and a, their; eclipse the initial consonants of their nouns (except p, on which they exert no influence), and prefix n to vowels; as áp ᴅ-ᴄíp, our country; ᴜap m-ba, your cows; a n-aċaɪp, their father.

6. Possessive pronouns amalgamated with prepositions (see p. 45) have the same influence over the initials of their nouns, as they have in their uncompounded state; as ᴅom ċroıṁe, to my heart; óna ᴅ-cír, from their country.

7. The manner of using the emphatic increase after the possessive pronouns has been already pointed out in Par. 3, page 45. For an additional Rule of possessives, see Rule 2, page 105.

III. RELATIVE PRONOUNS.

1. The relative follows its antecedent and precedes its verb; as an cé a ṗuıḃalṗaṗ, the person who shall walk.

2. The relative aspirates the initial of its verb; as an laoċ a ṁaṗḃ an c-aċaċ, "the hero who slew the giant." To this the next rule is an exception.

3. When the relative a signifies "all that" (see p. 47) it eclipses the initial of its verb; as a ḃ-ṗuıl ó Ġhaıllıḃ buṁ ṁeaṗ, "all that is from Galway southwards;" ᴅo ṗéıṗ a n-ᴅuḃṗamaṗ, "according to *what* we have said."

4. When the relative a is governed by a preposition, expressed or understood, and is followed immediately by a verb to which it is not the nominative, the initial of the verb (except ṗ) is eclipsed; as a ṗé mṁ ımoṗṗa ᴅá ᴅ-cáınıc a ḃáṗ "(the following) is the circumstance, indeed, *from which came* his death;" an ḃoıċ ına n-ıċıṁíṗ, "the tent in which they used to eat;" a ᴅuḃaıṗc Ṗıonn ɼo n-ᴅıonɼnaṁ (ṗíċ) ɼıṁ ḃé nóṗ a n-ᴅıonɼnaṁ Ṁıaṗmaıṁ í, "Finn said that he would make (peace) in whatever manner Diarmaid would make it" (here the preposition ann is understood:

ᚵıᴏ́ bé nóṗ ann a n-ᴏıonᵹnaᴏ́ Ⅾıaṗmaıᴏ́ í, whatever the manner *in which* Diarmaid would make it.) (See next rule).

5. If, in the case stated in the last rule, the verb is in the past tense, with the particle ṗo or ᴏo, the initial of the verb is not eclipsed, but aspirated (Pars. 1 and 4. p. 58); as ᴅıᴄ aṗ ᴄuıᴄ Ⅾaṗa Ⅾeaṗᵹ, "the place in which fell Dara Dearg"

6. The relative precedes the verb which governs it in the accusative (as in English); as an ᴄíṗ a ᵹṗaᴏ́uıᵹım, the country which I love.

7. As the relative has no inflection for case, the construction must determine whether the relative is the nominative to the verb which follows it, or is governed by it in the accusative; as an caṗa a ᵹṗaᴏ́uıᵹıᴏ́ mé, the friend whom I love; an caṗa a ᵹṗaᴏ́uıᵹeaṗ mé, the friend who loves me.

8. The relative is often omitted both in the nominative and in the accusative; as oᵹlaoċ ᴏo ṁuınnᴄıṗ Nín ṁıc Péıl ᴄaınıc uaıᴏ́ ᴏo ḃṗaċ na Eıṗıonn, "a youth of the people of Nin Mac Peil (who) came from him to view Erin." Ⅽn leaḃaṗ ṗo ṗcṗıoḃ (Caṁḃṗenṗıṗ) ᴏo ċuaṗaṗᵹḃaıl Eıṗıonn, "the book (which) Cambrensis wrote on the history of Erin."

9. The relative a is often disguised by combination with other words and particles, especially with ṗo, the mark of the past tense; as an ᴄíṗ óṗ ᴄáınıc me, "the country from which I came" (here óṗ = ó a ṗo); pláıᵹ léṗ maṗḃaᴏ́ noí míle ᴏ́íoḃ, "a plague, by which were killed nine thousand of them" (here léṗ = le a ṗo); an ᴄíṗ ᴏá ᴅ-ᴄáınıc ṗé, the country to which he came (ᴏá = ᴏo a), lá ᴏaṗ coṁóṗaᴏ́ aonaċ le ṗıᵹ Eıṗeann, "a day on which was convoked an assembly by the king of Erin" (ᴏaṗ = ᴏo a ṗo); ní beaᵹ ḣomṗa aṗ ḟloinneaṙ péin map eipic, "I do not think it little what I have named as an *eric*." (Ap=a ṗo, in which a means "all that:" Par. 3, page 47.)

IV. DEMONSTRATIVE PRONOUNS.

1. The demonstrative pronouns follow their nouns or pronouns; as an ṗeaṗ ṗın, that man; cia h-é ṗın? who is that?

Exception:—When the verb iṗ in any of its forms is understood; as ṗúḋ ḃaṗ ʒ-cuıḋ, "yonder (is) your meal;" ṗo an lá, this is the day.

2. If the noun be followed by one or more adjectives, the demonstrative pronoun comes last; as cia an ṗeaṗ ballaċ binnḃṗiaṫṗaċ úḋ? "Who is that freckled sweet-worded man?"

V. INTERROGATIVE AND INDEFINITE PRONOUNS.

1. An interrogative pronoun comes first in the sentence; as cá ḃ-ṗuil mo leaḃaṗ? where is my book? cia an laoċ úḋ aṗ ʒualainn Ꙟhoill? "who is that hero at the shoulder of Goll?"

This rule holds good even when the interrogative is governed by a preposition, i.e., the preposition follows the interrogative that it governs; as caḋ aṗ ṫu? out of what (place art) thou? ʒo ḃe maṗ ṫá ṫú? how do you do? (literally "like to what art thou?") cṗeuḋ ṗá an eiṗʒeaḃaṗ, "what for did ye rise?"

2. When uile precedes its noun, it means "every;" when it follows the noun it means "all;" as ṗlán ón uile ʒalaṗ, "sound from every sickness;" ḋa ḃaṫaḋ an cine ḋaona uile ʒo h-aon oċtaṗ, "all the human race was drowned, all to (except) a single eight."

There are occasional exceptions; as oṗonʒ ainḃṗioṗaḋ iṗ na h-uile ṗuḃáılaiḃ, "people ignorant in *all* virtues" (in this passage from Keating, uile means "all" though it precedes its noun).

CHAPTER VI.

THE VERB.

1. As a general rule the verb precedes its nominative; as do ġluaıꞃ Ƒeꞃʒuꞃ, "Fergus went;" do claoıðcað Mac Ɉaꞃꞃaıð, "Mac Garraidh was defeated." (See next Rule.)

2. When the nominative is a relative or an interrogative pronoun, it precedes the verb; and sometimes also in poetry, the nominative, even though a noun, precedes the verb; as an ꞇe a ꞃıubalꞅaꞃ, the person who will walk; cꞃeud aꞇá annꞅo? what is here? Deóꞃaıðꞇe ꞃíoꞃa ʒan ꞃʒıꞇ ʒan ꞃoꞃ míanaıd a d-ꞇíꞃ 'ꞅ a n-dúꞇċaꞃ, "perpetual exiles without pause or rest, long-for their country and their native-home."

3. When the verb is transitive, i.e., when it governs the accusative (see Rule 9, p. 111), the usual order is verb, nominative, object; as do aıʒel Conċobaꞃ boꞃaċ, "Conchobhar addressed Borach;" do líon Ɉꞃáınne an coꞃn, "Grainne filled the goblet."

4. But when the accusative is a relative or an interrogative pronoun, the usual order is, pronoun (or accusative), verb, nominative; as an laoċ a ċonaıꞃc mé ané, the hero *whom I saw* yesterday; cad deıꞃ ꞇú? what sayest thou?

5. When the verb ꞇá is used, the usual order is, verb, nominative, predicate; as ꞇáıd na ꞃeulꞇa ꞃo-lonnꞃaċ, the stars are very bright.

6. When the verb ıꞅ, expressed or understood, is used, the usual order is, verb, predicate, nominative; as ba bınne a ʒlóꞃ ná ceól na n-éun, "*her voice* *was sweeter* than the music of the birds:" ní ṗaḋa uaiṫ an ḋiṫ, " not (is) far from thee the place."

Exception.—If the article is used before the predicate, or if the predicate is a proper name, the order is, verb, subject, predicate; as iṗ ṫuṗa an ṫíṗ ṗo-aoiḃinn, "thou art the delightful country;" iṗ mé Cían mac Cáinṫe, "I am Cian, the son of Cainte:" an ṫu Ḟionn? "art thou Finn?"

7. The only cases in which there is agreement between the verb and its nominative, are (1) when the nominative and verb are both third person singular; (2) when a noun or pronoun in third plural has a verb in third plural, in accordance with Par. 9, p. 50.

It may be doubted whether (1) is a genuine case of agreement; and the general absence of agreement between verb and nominative is further exemplified in the following rule.

8. When two or more nouns, whether singular or plural, joined by a conjunction, are nominatives to one verb, the verb has the third person singular form; as ḋo ġluaiṗ bṗeaṗ aġuṗ na ḋṗaoiṫe ṗómpa, "Breas and the druids went forward."

9. A transitive verb governs the noun or pronoun which is the object of the action, in the accusative case; as buail é, strike him; ḋo ċuiṗeaḋaṗ Ṫuaṫa Ḋe Ḋanann ceó ḋṗaoiḋeaċṫa i n-a ḃ-ṫimċeall ṗéin, "the Tuatha de Dananns *put* a magical *mist* around themselves."

10. The initial of a verb in the infinitive mood is aspirated, unless the aspiration is prevented by some special influence. For such an influence see Par. 2, p. 60.

11. The preposition le or ṗe before the infinitive active often gives it a passive signification; as (leaḃaiṗ eile) aṫá ṗe ḃ-ṗaicṗin i n-Ciṗinn, "(other books, which are *to be seen* in Erin."

But in many such constructions the preposition expresses purpose, and the signification is active; as aġuṗ ġo m-biḋ ollaṁ ṗe ḃénaṁ ṗeille uṗ a ċéile, " and that they are ready *to do* treachery on each other."

12. The infinitive, even without the preposition to, has often a passive signification; as Ḟiaċra mac Ailene tiġearna Muġḋorn do marḃaḋ, "Fiachra, son of Ailene, lord of Mourne, to be slain" (lit. "Fiachra, &c., to slay"): aġur an ꝼear naċ tioḃraḋ (an cíor) rin uaiḋ, a ṡrón do ḃuain óna ċeann de, "and the man who would not pay that tribute from him, his nose *to be cut* off from his head."

13. One verb governs another that follows it or depends upon it in the infinitive mood; as da m-baḋ naċ raċraḋ clanna Mornne d'iarraiḋ na ġ-caor rin, "if it were so that the Clann Morna *had not come to seek* those berries."

The following very important rule was first enunciated by O'Donovan, and is given here in his own words ("Irish Grammar," p. 387.)

14. "When the governed verb is one expressing motion or gesture, which does not govern the accusative, the sign do is never prefixed; as duḃairt ré liom dul ġo Corcaiġ, he told me to go to Cork."

15. If the noun which is the object of a transitive verb in the infinitive mood follows the verb, it is in the genitive case; as tanġadar caḃlaċ mór do ḋéanaṁ coġuiḋ, "a great fleet came *to make war*" (nom. coġaḋ, war, gen. coġuiḋ); do ṁilleaḋ cloinne Lir, "to kill the children of Lir."

16. A noun or pronoun which is the object of a transitive verb in the infinitive mood often precedes the verb, and in this case it is (not in the genitive, as in the last rule, but) in the accusative; as, aġur ireaḋ do ġníoḋ, dá ċuaille do ċur i d-talṁain aġur ceann an t-rnáite do ċeanġal da ġaċ cuaille díoḃ, aġur uḃall do ċur air ṁullaċ cuaille aca, "and it is what he used to do, *two poles to put* in the earth, and *the end* of a thread *to tie* to each pole of them, and *an apple to put* on the top of a pole of them."

17. The active participle of a transitive verb governs the noun which is the object of the action, in the genitive case; as ag bpuicneaḋ an óip, "smelting the gold" (lit. "smelting of the gold"); do ḃí an Ġaoḋal ro ag múnaḋ rcol, "this Gaodhal was teaching schools" (lit. "teaching of schools"); ag coċailc na calṁan, "digging the ground."

18. The verb ip in any of its forms expressed or understood, takes the accusative form of a personal pronoun as its nominative; as ip í céaḋpaḋ ḋpoinge re reanċup, "*it* is the opinion of some historians;" ip mic pig go pípinneaċ iaḋ, "*they* are truly sons of a king;" agup pıappaıġear an piġ cia h-iaḋ péin, "and the king asks who *they* (are)."

19. The verb ip is very often omitted, especially in negative and interrogative sentences, and in answers to questions; as beaċa an pcapaiḋe pípinne, "truth (is) the food of the historian;" ceann Ḋiapmuḋa Uı Ḋhuıḃne an ceann úḋ, "that head (is) the head of Diarmaid O'Duibhne;" cia cupa? mipı Iollan, "who (art) thou? I (am) Iollan;" an píop pın, "whether (is) that true? ní mipı, "(it is) not I."

20. A verb in the passive voice takes the accusative form of a personal pronoun as its nominative; as ḋéancap é, it is done; buaılceap ıaḋ they are struck.

CHAPTER VII.

PREPOSITIONS.

1. A simple preposition governs the dative (including the ablative, for which there is no distinct inflection); as τάinic ré 5o Copcais, he came *to Cork;* a5 coip an t-pléibe, *at the foot* of the mountain; aipíıo cuıo be na h-ú5oapaıb, "some *of the authors* reckon." (See next rule for exception.)

2. The preposition ιοιρ generally governs the accusative in the singular, and the dative in the plural; as ιοιρ Copcac a5up Luımneac, between Cork and Limerick; ιοιρ na córseaoaıb, "between the provinces."

3. The prepositions ann, 5o, ıap, pıa, le or pe, and tap, take p before an, the article, the p being sometimes joined with the preposition and sometimes with the article; as annp an leaoap or ann pan leaoap, in the book; leip an b-peap, with the man. (See par. 7, page 17.)

4. The compound prepositions govern their nouns in the genitive; as bo pu5 an conna pıp a n-a5aıo an cnuıc, "he brought the tun with him *against the hill;*" a b-pıaonuıpe b-peap n-Cıpıonn, "*in presence of the men* of Erin;" bo 5luaıpeaoap clann Cuıpeann pompa o'ıonnpuıoc an caca, "the children of Tuireann went forwards *towards the battle.*"

The following prepositions, cum, towards; bála, as to; béıp, after; ıomcupa, as to; meap5 or aıneap5, amongst; péıp, according to; and cımcıoll, about, although having the form of simple prepositions, are in reality compound, and take their nouns in the genitive. See end of Par. 3, p. 83.

As a compound preposition consists of a noun governed by a simple preposition, it is in reality the noun-part of the compound preposition that governs the noun in the genitive, in accordance with Rule 1, page 95: thus the expression above, a n-a5aıo an cnuıc, is literally "in the face of the hill," where cnuıc is governed in the genitive by a5aıo, face; and so of the others.

5. The simple prepositions, except bo, be, 5an, and ıoıp, generally cause eclipsis in singular nouns when the article is used; as ó'n 5-cnoc pın, "from

that hill;" ᴀᴢ an m-baile na h-inre riar, "at the town of the island in the west." (See pages 17, 18.)

6. The simple prepositions generally cause aspiration when the article is not expressed; as air barr an croinn, "on the top of the tree;" ó múraib na Teamrac, "from the ramparts of Tara."

Exception 1: a or i, iar, and ᴢo (when it means "with") cause eclipsis without the article; as a m-baile ata cliat, in Baile-atha-cliath (Dublin); iar n-bílinn, "after the deluge."

Exception 2: aᴢ. le, and sometimes ᴢo, cause no change in the initial, and ᴢan may either aspirate or not; as rlán le Maiᴢ, "farewell to (the river) Maigue;" o'n t-Sionuinn roir ᴢo rairrᴢe, "from the Shannon east *to the sea*."

7. When a simple preposition ending in a vowel comes before the possessive a (whether it signifies *his, her,* or *their*), the letter n is inserted between the vowels; as tre n-a baraib, "*through his* hands;" an lá ᴢo n-a lán t-roillre, "the day *with its* abundant light."

Except after do and de; as tabair féur dá capall give grass to his horse; bain ᴢeuᴢ d'á ᴢ-crann, take a branch from their tree.

Before any other word beginning with a vowel, the letter h is usually inserted after these prepositions; as do cuaᴅ re ᴢo h-Albain, he went to Alban (Scotland).

PART IV.
IDIOMS.

An idiom, in the sense in which it is used here, may be defined:—An expression that has acquired by usage a certain meaning, which becomes lost in a word-for-word translation into another language; so that in order to convey the true meaning in that other language, the form of expression must be changed.

Thus, "tá an leabap aʒ an buine" is an idiom, for its sense is lost in the word-for-word translation, "the book is at the man;" and in order to convey the true meaning, the English expression must be changed to "the man has the book."

Idioms constitute one of the chief difficulties in learning any language; and the student is recommended to master this Part, in which the principal idioms of the Irish language are explained and illustrated.

1. The Infinitive governing Possessive Pronouns.

The infinitive of a transitive verb governs its object in the genitive (Syntax, Rule 15, p. 112). When the object, instead of being a noun, is a personal pronoun, then, according to the analogy of the Rule quoted, it should be in the genitive case. But the genitive of a personal pronoun is a possessive pronoun; and possessive pronouns precede the words they refer to; so that the pronoun which represents the object of the action, is a possessive, and precedes the infinitive, influencing its initial as if it were a noun (see Syntax, p. 106, Rules 3, 4, 5). This gives rise to idiomatic expressions like the following, which are of very frequent occurrence.

	English.	Irish.	Contracted to.
To strike	me,	do mo bualaḋ,	dom' bualaḋ.
	thee,	do do bualaḋ,	dod' bualaḋ.
	him,	do a bualaḋ,	dá bualaḋ.
	her,	do a bualaḋ,	dá bualaḋ.
	us,	do áp m-bualaḋ,	dáp m-bualaḋ.
	you,	do bup m-bualaḋ,	(not contracted)
	them,	do a m-bualaḋ,	dá m-bualaḋ.

PART IV.]   IDIOMS.   117

These may be translated literally, "to my striking," "to their striking," &c.

A like construction prevails in the case of a transitive participle: aᵹ a ḃualaḋ, striking him: aᵹ a ḃualaḋ, striking her: aᵹ án m-ḃualaḋ, striking us, &c. In this construction the participle may itself be governed in the genitive case by a noun :—ċáinic mían a maṗḃċa ḃam ṗéin, "a desire to kill them, has come to me" (lit. " a desire of the killing of them," or " of their killing.")

2. Compound Prepositions governing Possessive Pronouns.

A compound preposition governs the genitive (Rule 4, p. 114); and when the governed word is not a noun but a personal pronoun, this last becomes a possessive, and goes before the noun-part of the compound preposition, giving rise to idiomatic phrases, corresponding with those quoted in last Idiom. Example: aiṗ ṗon, for the sake ᴊ"; aiṗ a ṗon, for his sake; aiṗ ḃuṗ ṗon, for your sake, &c. Do ċuaiḋ Diaṗmaiḋ ḋá h-éiṗ, Diarmaid went after her: ċáinic cinneaṗ oṗṗa ṗein, aᵹuṗ aṗ a ṗhoċċ 'n-a n-ḃiaiḋ. " sickness came upon themselves, and on their posterity after them."

A similar construction often occurs with the compound adverbs. Example: caṗ aiṗ, backwards; do ċuaiḋ ṗé caṗ a aiṗ, he went backwards; do ċuaiḋ ṗí caṗ a h-aiṗ, she went backwards; do ċuaiḋ ṗiaḋ caṗ a n-aiṗ, they went backwards, &c.

3. To die.

"To die," is very often expressed in Irish by a phrase meaning "to find death:" the verb ṗaᵹ, find, being used for this purpose, in its various forms; as, an ḃaṗa ḃliaᵹain ḋá éiṗ ṗin ṗuaiṗ Iṗial ḃáṗ, "the second year after that Irial *found death ;*" aᵹuṗ máṗ ann acá a n-ḃán ḃaiṁ ḃáṗ ḃ'ṗáᵹail, "and if it be here that it is in fate for me death to find" (i. e., "that it is fated for me to die.")

There is, however, a single verb ḃ'euᵹ, meaning to die, but it is not used so often as the above. The following example exhibits both forms:—A ḃeiṗ cuiḋ ḃo na ṗean-uᵹḃaṗaiḃ ᵹuṗ aḃ a nᵹleann ḃa loċa ṗuaiṗ naoṁ Paḃ-ṗuiᵹ ḃáṗ; ḃioḋ ᵹo n-aḃṗaiḋ ḃṗunᵹ oile ᵹuṗaḃ ann

Apómaċa b'eug pó, "some of the old authors say that it is in Glendalough St. Patrick found death, although another party say that it is in Armagh he died."

4. Nominative Absolute.

What is called the nominative absolute in English is expressed in Irish by the preposition aıp (on), or ıap (after), placed before the participle, and the preposition do (to) before the noun; which will be understood from the following examples.—aп m-beıċ aċa paḋa do Chopmac aġ a ḃ-peıċıoṁ, "Cormac, having been a long time watching them" (lit. "on being a long time to Cormac a-watching of them"): aġup aıp m-beıċ ollaṁ don luıng, "and the ship being ready" (lit. "and on being ready to the ship"); aġup aıp n-dul a luıng dóıḃ, "and they having gone into a ship:" (lit. "and on going into a ship to them"): ıap m-beıċ ċpéan ıp an ċíp dóıḃ, "they having grown strong in the country" (lit. "after being strong in the country to them").

5. To have no help for a thing.

The Irish phrase corresponding to this is "to have no strength (neapċ) on a thing:" the "having" being expressed in accordance with Idiom 34, p 130. Ní ḃ-puıl neapċ aġum aıp an nıḋ pın, I have no help for that thing—I cannot help that (lit. "there is to me no strength on that thing"). Aġup a duḃaıpċ Ġpáınne naċ paıḃ neapċ aıce péın aıp, "and Grainne said that she had no help for it" (or "could not help it," "could not have prevented it"). Sometimes léıġeap, remedy or cure, is used in the same way as neapċ.

6. To cause a thing to be done.

To cause a thing to be done, to have it done, to see that it is done, to order it to be done, is often expressed in Irish by do ċup (or do ċaḃaıpċ) pá ḋeapa, "to put (or bring, or give), under notice." Aġup po ċuıp Mıoḋaċ pa n-ḋeapa úıp Inıp Tuıle do ċup púıḃ, "and Miodhach caused the mould (or soil) of Inis Tuile to be placed under you:" do pug (píġ) bpeaċ báıp aıp an m-bpeıċeam, aġup ċug pa ḋeapa a ċpoċaḋ "(the king), passed sentence of death on the judge, and had him hanged" ("put under notice him to hang," or "his hanging").

7. Number of individuals of which a company is composed.

The number of individuals of which any collection of persons or things is made up, is often inserted, in the nominative form, in a narrative sentence, without any syntactical connexion with the rest of the sentence. Aҙur ċainic ụp ṗóṁe arnamáraḋ, caoҕac caippċcaḋ, ó Shíoc buiḋḃ Ṽeiрҕ. "and Lir set out on the morrow, fifty chariot-men, from Shee Bove Derg" (i.e., *with* fifty chariots): aҙur caimic boḋḃ Ṽearҕ, naoi céaḋ piċċeaḋ, ḋa n-ionnruiċe; "and Bove Derg came, twenty-nine hundred men, towards them."

This is like the English :—"The duke began his march next morning, 20,000 strong."

8. Passive Verbs used impersonally.

A passive verb is often used impersonally; as ҕaḃra ḋuҕainn amaċ, aҙur ní laṁrap ruiliuҕaḋ orc, "come forth to us and no one will dare to wound thee :" (literally, "and *it will not be dared* [to put] wounding on thee).

This form of expression is of very frequent occurrence in the older narrative writings :—thus instead of "they advance; they plunge into the (river) Crond," the writer expresses himself in this way :—"it is advanced; it is plunged into the Crond."

9. Nominatives before Infinitives and Participles.

Instead of the usual assertive construction, consisting of a verb with its nominative (noun or pronoun), the following construction is often adopted :—the verb is put in the infinitive or participial form, and the subject (whether noun or personal pronoun) is placed before it, the pronoun being in the accusative form (but whether the noun is nominative or accusative cannot be determined, as there is no distinction of form); as ir aṁlaiḋ ḃí Nairi aҙur Ṽeirḋre, aҙur an ċennċaiṁ ecarra, aҙur iaḋ aҕ imirc uirre, "it is in this manner Naisi and Deirdre were (seated), and the Cennchaimh (a chess board) between them, *and they playing on it;* ir aṁlaiḋ ḋo ḃí Coḃċaċ, aҙur é aҕ rearҕaḋ, "it is thus Cobhthach was, *and he* pining away ;" cuirior rceula ҕo ḃláċnuiḋ é féin ḋo ḃeiċ ann rin, "he sends word to Blanid, *he* himself *to be* there" (i.e., "that he himself was there").

120 IDIOMS. [PART IV

This form of expression is often adopted even when the verb or participle is (not expressed but) understood; as do cuip (an cú) a ceann a n-ucc Ḋiaṛmuda aġuṛ é ina ċoḋla "(the hound) put her head in the breast of Diarmaid, *and he in his sleep.*"

10. One person meeting another.

"Donall met Fergus" is often expressed in Irish in the following way:—Do caṛaḋ Ḟeṛġuṛ aiṛ Ḋoṁnall; literally "Fergus was met (or turned) on Donall." Do caṛaḋ Aoiḃell na Cṛaiġe léiṫċ oṛuinn, "we met Eevel of Craglea" (lit. "Eevel of Craglea was met [or turned] on us"): cia caṛṛaiḋe oṛm aċċ ṛuaiḋ-bean, "whom should I meet but the fair woman" ("who should be met on me").
The same idea is expressed by the verb ṫaṛla, happened: aġuṛ ṫáṛla oġlaċ oṛṛṫa aṛ m-boġaċ, "and they met a youth on the moor" (lit. "and a youth happened on [or to] them") ṫṛiallluiḋ ġo Sliab Miṛ ġo ṫṫáṛla banba ġo n-a ḃṛaoiṫiḃ oṛṛa ann, "they travel to Slieve Mish until they met Banba with her druids there" ("until Banba with her druids happened on[or to] them there").

11. Although: Although not.

Ġion ġo or ġion ġuṛ has two opposite meanings which can only be distinguished by the general sense of the passage: sometimes it means "although" (or "although that"), and sometimes "although not."
Although:—a Ḟhinn, aṛ Oṛġaṛ, ġion ġuṛ ḟoiġṛe mo ġaol ḋuiṫṛe ná do Ḋiaṛmuiḋ O Ḋhuiḃne, "'O Finn, says Oscar, 'although my relationship with thee is nearer than to Diarmaid O'Duibhne.'"
Although not:—do ḃéṛuim cóṁaiṛle ṁaiṫ ḋíḃ, a Chlann Uiṛniġ, ġion ġo n-ḃénċaṛ liḃ í, "I shall give a good counsel to you, O sons of Usna, though it will not be done by you," ġion ġuṛ ċeáṛṛḃ mná an níṫ ṛin, "*although* that proceeding would *not* be the business of a woman."

12. To be able.

To be able to do a thing is expressed in different ways. The most usual is by phrases of the type, iṛ ḟéiḋiṛ le, "it is possible with," as iṛ ḟéiḋiṛ l'om a ḋéanaḋ, I can do it (lit. "it is possible with me to do it:" see Idiom 1.)
Another, and more idiomatic way, is by the verb ṫiġim, " I

come," in its various moods and tenses; and with this verb "I can do," or "I am able to do," is expressed by "it comes with me to do;" as muna b-τιʒeaḋ ꝑiꞃ an ċailleaċ b'amaꞃ, "unless he would be able to strike the hag" (lit. "unless it would come with him the hag to strike"); aċτ nioꞃ ḃoilʒe ꝑinn ina ꞃin maꞃ aτáiḋ áꞃ b-τꞃí ꝑéinniḋe ceanʒailτe ináꞃ ḃ-ꝑiaḋnuiꞃe, aʒuꞃ naċ b-τiʒ ꝑinn ꞃʒaoileaḋ ḋíoḃ, "and we think more grievous than that, how our three champions are bound in our presence, and that we are not able to free them:" ní ċuiꞃeann ualaċ oꞃꞃainn naċ b-τiʒ linn a iomċaꞃ, "he puts not a burden on us that we are not able to bear."

Sometimes the verb τá or iꞃ is used instead of τiʒ, and also the preposition aʒ instead of le; as ó naċ liom ḃul ón ʒ-conτaḃaiꞃτ ꞃo, "since I cannot escape from this danger" ("since it *is* not with me to go from this danger": here iꞃ is understood): ó naċ ḃ-ꝑuil ḃul uaiḋ aʒum, "since I cannot escape from him" ("since it is not with me to go from him:" here τá and aʒ are used, as in "possession:" Idiom 34.

13. One of a pair.

One of a pair is often expressed by the word leaċ, half: leaċ-ċoꞃ, one foot (lit. half-foot). In this compound the word leaċ is used adjectively, so that leaċ-ċoꞃ means, not half *of* a foot, but a *half*-foot (i.e., a foot which is itself a half, i.e., half of a pair). So also leaċ-ꞃúil, one eye, leaċ-τaoḃ, one side, &c. Iꞃ amlaiḋ ḃo ḃí an ꞃiʒ ꞃin aʒuꞃ leaċ-lam aiꞃʒiḋ aiꞃ, "it is thus that king was, and one hand of silver on him."

14. To be alone.

The word aonaꞃ, which the dictionaries now interpret as meaning "alone," was originally a concrete numeral noun like τꞃiúꞃ, cúiʒeaꞃ, &c. (p. 39), and meant "one person;" and this meaning it retains to some extent in its present application:—ḃo ꞃiuḃal mé a'm aonaꞃ, I walked alone (lit. "I walked in my one person" [see Idiom 42]: or "I walked as one person"); ḃo ꞃiuḃal τú aḃ' aonaꞃ, thou walkedst alone: ḃo ꞃiuḃal ꞃí n-a h-aonaꞃ, "she walked alone," &c.; am aonaꞃ ꞃeal a ꞃiuḃal ḃiḋeaꞃ, "alone, of a time, walking I was."

Another way of saying in Irish "he is alone" is "he is with himself:" τá mé liom ꝑéin, I am alone ("I am with myself"): τá τú leaτ ꝑéin, thou art alone: τá ꞃiaḋ leo ꝑéin, they are alone: τá mo máτꞃín 'n-a coḃlaḋ, aʒuꞃ muiꞃe liom ꝑéin, "my mother is asleep, and I am alone."

15. One thing given for another.

When you give or take, sell or buy, one thing for another, it is expressed in Irish by saying you give it, &c., *on* that other, the preposition ɑıɲ being used. Ꝺo ċuɡ ɼé cɲí ƀɑ ɑıɲ ɑn ɡ-cɑpɑll ɼın, he gave three cows for that horse: ɑıɲ Ҽıɲe ní 'neóɲɑınn cıɑ h-í, "for Erin I would not tell who she is" ('neóɲɑınn for ınneóɲɑınn: see p. 63).

In this sense, the preposition ɑıɲ is set before the noun of price: ꝺo ċeɑnnuıɡeɑɼ ɑn ƀó ƀán ɼın ɑıɲ ɼé púınc. I bought that white cow for six pounds: ní h-ıonɡnɑ ɑɲ Coɲmɑc, óıɲ ıɼ mɑıċ ɑn luɑċ cuɡɑɼ uıɲɲe, "'No wonder,' says Cormac, 'for good is the price I gave for it.'"

16. Debt.

The fact that Donall owes Fergus money, or that Donall is under any obligation to pay money to Fergus, is expressed by saying, "Fergus has money on Donall," the preposition ɑıɲ being used before the name of the debtor, and the act of "having" being expressed by cá and ɑɡ as in Idiom 34. Cá cɲí púınc ɑɡ Ƒeɲɡuɼ ɑıɲ Ꝺoṁnɑll, Donall owes three pounds to Fergus: cá beɑn eıle ɑ n-Ҽoċɑıll ɑ ƀ-ꝼuıl ɑıcı coɲóın ɑıɲ, there is another woman in Youghal to whom he owes a crown" ("to whom is a crown on him"): ıɼ ɑṁlɑıꝺ ꝺo ƀí ɑn ɲíɡ ɼo, ɑɡuɼ cıoɼ cáın móɲ cɲom ɑɡ Ƒoıhoɲɑıɡ ɑɲ Ϲuɑċɑ Ꝺé Ꝺɑnɑnn ɲe n-ɑ lınn, "it is how this king was, and (that) the Fomorians had a great heavy tribute and rule over the Tuatha De Dananns during his time" ("a great heavy tribute and rule was with the Fomorians on the Tuath De Dananns").

17. Asking, entreating, &c.

To ask, request, entreat, or demand of a person, is expressed by "to ask, &c., *on* that person:" ıɑɲɲ ɑıɲ Ꝺhıɑ nɑ ɡɲáɼɑ ɼın, "ask of God those graces."

18. Sensation, suffering, &c.

That a person is hungry, thirsty, cold, afraid, sick, &c., is expressed in Irish by saying that hunger, thirst, cold, fear, sickness, &c., is *on* him, the preposition ɑıɲ being used: cá ꝼuɑċc oɲm (cold is on me), I am cold; ná bíoꝺ eɑɡlɑ oɲc (let not fear be on thee) be not afraid: ꝺo ƀí cɑɲc móɲ ɑıɲ Sheɑ-ɡɑn (great thirst was on John), John was very thirsty; cɑꞇ

PART IV.] IDIOMS. 123

é ſin orṫ? (what is that on thee?) what ails you? A ċuiple
mo ċroiḋe creuḋ í an ġruaim ſin orṫ? "O pulse of my
heart, what is that frown on thee?"

19. One person entertaining feelings (of love, hatred, &c.) towards another.

That Donall entertains certain feelings towards Fergus is expressed by saying that Donall *has* such feelings *on* Fergus; the preposition aiſ being used before "Fergus," and the act of "having" being expressed by tá and aġ, as in idiom 34:—ní mó an cion ro bá aġ Aonġus orcra ind an cion ro bá aġ muincir Aonġura ar ṁac an reaċcaine. ġo raiḃ formaḋ mór ar t'aṫair fá n-a ċionn ſin, "not greater was the affection Aonghus felt for thee than the affection the people of Aonghus felt for the son of the steward, so that thy father felt great jealousy on that account" (lit. "not greater was the affection which was with Aonghus on thee, ... so that great jealousy was on thy father on the head of that:" see Idiom 32).

Where the agent is not specified, a similar form of expression is retained: you are loved, is expressed by love is on you: you are esteemed, by estimation is on you, &c.: tá meaſ aġur cion mór air Orcar (great esteem and love are on Oscar), Oscar is greatly *esteemed and loved*.

20. To know: to know a person.

To know is usually expressed in Irish by the phrase knowledge is with me, I have knowledge; and to know a person by "to have or to give knowledge on a person:" "'aġur an ḃ-ſuil a ſior aġaḋ ſéin, a Ḟinn?' 'ní ḃ-ſuil,' an Ḟionn:" "'do you know it, O Finn?' 'I do not,' says Finn" (lit., is its knowledge with you, O Finn? It is not, says Finn): an áil leat ſior ḋ'ſáġail? do you wish to know? ("is it a desire with you knowledge to get?"): bioḋ a ſior aġat, a leuġtóir. "know O reader" ("be its knowledge with thee, O reader"): (strangers are seen coming towards Finn and his party), ro ſiarraiġ Ḟionn do ċáċ an ḃ-tuġaḋar aiṫne orrta, "Finn asked of the others did they know them" (lit. "did they put knowledge on them"): aġur tuġairre aiṫne orm, "and thou knewest ɾe ' (lit. "and thou didst put knowledge on me").

124   IDIOMS.   [PART IV.

21. To part from, to separate from.

To separate from a person is expressed in Irish by "to separate *with* a person," the preposition le or ꞃe being used: much in the same manner as we say in English, "I parted with him:" ꞃcaꞃaḃaꞃ ꞃéin aᵹuꞃ Ḋiaꞃmaiḋ ꞃe n-a ċéile, "they themselves and Diarmaid separated from each other:" ḋo ꞃcaꞃ ꞃé ꞃinn, "he separated from us;" ꞃcaꞃ Oꞃcaꞃ le Ḋiaꞃmaiḋ, "Oscar separated from Diarmaid:" ḋo ꞃcaꞃ ꞃiꞃ, "he separated from him;" aᵹ Cuꞃꞃaċ Ċill'-ḋaꞃa ḋo ꞃcaꞃaꞃ le ᵹꞃaḋ mo ċꞃoiḋe, "at the Curragh of Kildare I parted from the 'love of my heart.'"

22. However great, however good, however brave, &c.

Ḋa placed before some abstract nouns gives a meaning which, though it is well understood in practical use, has puzzled grammarians to analyse and explain, and which will be best understood by a few examples. From the adjective álainn, fine or beautiful, is formed áilne or áille, fineness, beauty; and ḋa áilne or ḋa áille, means "however fine," "how fine soever." Examples:—Ní ḃ-ꞃuil pionúꞃ ḃá ṁeuḋ,naċ ḃ-cuillib, "there is no punishment however great that they do not deserve:" an cꞃeaꞃ ᵹeiꞃ, ᵹan coṁꞃaᵹ aoinꞅiꞃ ḃá cꞃéiꞃi aiꞃ calṁain ḋ'oḃaḋ, "the third injunction, not to refuse single combat to any man on earth, however mighty:" ḋeaṁan ná ḋiaḃal ḃá cꞃéiꞃe láṁ, "demon or devil, however mighty of hand."

23. Both one and another: both these and those.

Both, in such phrases as "both men and women," is often expressed in Irish by the preposition iḋiꞃ, between; as ḃainꞅiḋ Ḋia ꞃáꞃaṁ ḋioḃ ann ᵹaċ ꞃoċaꞃ ḋ'á ḃ-cuᵹ ḋóiḃ iḋiꞃ ċeill, ceaḋꞃaḋaiḃ, aᵹuꞃ conaċ ꞃaoᵹalca, "God will exact an account from them in every advantage He has given to them *between* understanding, senses, and worldly prosperity:" cúiᵹ. ṁíle iḋiꞃ ꞃeaꞃaiḃ aᵹuꞃ mnáiḃ, five thousand, between men and women (i.e. both men and women, or reckoning men and women).

24. To overtake.

To overtake a person is often expressed by "to bear on a person," the verb ḃeiꞃ, bear, being used with the preposition aıɼ. Examples:—Ḟáġḃam an culaḋ ɼo aɼ eaɼla ɼo m-beaɼɼaḋ Aonġuɼ an Ḃɼoġa oɼɼuınn, "let us leave this hill for fear that Aonghus of the Brugh would overtake us:" leanuɼ aıɼ a loɼɼ ɼo ɼéıṁóıɼeaḋ ıaḋ ḋo'n Ṁhúṁaın, ɼo ɼuɼ oɼɼa aɼ Solḋóıḋ, "he follows them on their track directly to Munster, so that he overtook them at Solchoid:" ɼo naḋ ɼúıɼɼıḋíɼ an ɼonn ɼın nó ɼo m-beıɼeaḋ Ṁaɼcɼa Síḋe oɼɼa, "that they might not leave that territory till the fairy cavalcade should overtake them:" ɼanɼaḋɼa leac aɼ an láṫaıɼ ɼo nó ɼo m-beıɼıɼ oɼm aɼíɼ, "I will wait for thee at this place till thou overtake me again:" ɼaḋ aon aıɼ a m-béaɼɼaınnɼı, "every one whom I would overtake" ("every one on whom I would bear").

25. To win a game on a person.

To win a game on a person is expressed by "to put a game on him:" aɼuɼ ḋo ṫóɼ Oıɼín an ɼeaɼ ɼın, aɼuɼ ɼo ḋuıɼ an cluıṫċe aɼ Ḟıonn, "and Oisin moved that (chess-) man and won a game on Finn:" aɼuɼ ní ɼuɼaman an báıɼe aɼ a ċéıle, "and we did not win the goal on each other" (i.e. neither of us won the goal on the other."

26. To think long, short, well of, ill of: to think hot, cold, hateful, &c.

Such phrases as "it seemed long to him," "he thought it long," are expressed by the verb ıɼ and the preposition le: ıɼ ɼaḋa lıom ("it is long with me"), it seems long to me, I think it long. Aɼuɼ ḋo ḃo ɼaḋa le na ḃɼáıṫɼıḃ ḋo ḃí Ḃɼıan uaṫa, "and his brothers thought it long that Brian was away from them" ("it was long with his brothers, &c."): ıɼ olc lınn an ḃean ɼıoc, "we think bad of what has happened to thee" ("it is evil with us:" aɼ = a ɼo, and a means "all that:" see p. 47): cuıɼımɼı naḋ ıoníhuın leacɼa me ɼéın, "I understand that thou dost not love me" ("that not beloved with thee am I myself").

Observe the difference in meaning conveyed by the two prepositions le and ḋo: ıɼ maıṫ é ḋo'n ḃ-ɼeaɼ ɼın, it is advantageous to that man (whether he thinks it so or not): ıɼ maıṫ é leıɼ an ḃ-ɼeaɼ ɼın, that man thinks it advantageous (whether it is really so or not). The following example shows both forms:—ba ṁaıṫ lıom ɼıuḃaıl aḋṫ nıoɼ ṁaıṫ ḋam é, I wished to walk, but it was not good for me.

126   IDIOMS.   [PART IV.

27. To wish for: to like: to be glad of: to prefer.

After the same manner, a desire, wish, liking for, &c., if expressed by such words as mian, desire; aiṫ, pleasure; áil, will or pleasure, &c.: ɪf áill liom fios d'fáġail, I wish to know ("it is a desire with me knowledge to get"): do ċuiɼfinn féin fúil an ċaiṫ ɼin aḋ h-uċṫ a n-ionaḋ do fúl, aɼ feaɼ díoḃ: do ḃ'aiṫ liom ɼin, aɼ an dóirseoir, "'I would put the eye of that cat in thy lap in place of thy eye,' says a man of them. 'I would like that,' says the door-keeper."

The word feáɼɼ, better, is used in the same way to express preference: ɪf feáɼɼ liom do ḋeaɼḃɼáṫair ná ṫusa, I prefer thy brother to thyself: I would rather have thy brother than thyself (lit. "thy brother is better with me," &c.); do ḃ'feáɼɼ le Briġid leaḃaɼ maiṫ ná airgead Brigid would prefer a good book to money (lit. "a good book would be better with Brigid," &c.). The following example shows the application of both mian and feáɼɼ:—Ní h-é if mian leiɼ an uġdaɼ (ní mo, ní h-é if mian liom-ɼa) ṫu do ḃreuġaṫ; . . . . aċṫ if é doḃ' feáɼɼ leiɼ ɼin (agur liom-ɼa) do ċroiḋe do feaḃuġaḋ: "it is not what the author wishes (neither is it my wish) to amuse thee (ṫu do ḃreuġaṫ) . . . . but it is what he would prefer (and I also) to possess thy heart."

Feáɼɼ followed by le expresses mental preference as shown above: but feáɼɼ followed by do is equivalent to the English expression "better for," "better that," &c. Ir feáɼɼ dómra anoir, aɼ Luġ, fios na h-eaɼca úḋ do ṫabairṫ daoiḃ. Ir feáɼɼ ċeana, aɼ iaḋɼan, 'it is *better for me* now,' says Lugh, 'a knowledge of that *eric* (fine) to give you.' 'It is better indeed,' say they."

28. To think little of—much of—to grudge.

Similar to the preceding is the use of the words beag and móɼ (little and much) in several idiomatic phrases, which occur very frequently, and which will be best understood by the following examples:—Ir móɼ liom an luaċ ɼin, I think that price large ("that price is large with me"): óir dá m-beiṫ mac aguinne iona fuiḋe rompa, níoɼ ḃeag leo do ċuir dár marḃaḋ é, "for if (even) a child of us would be sitting ("in his sitting:" see Idiom 42) before them, they would not deem it (too) little cause to kill us" (lit. "it would not be with them a small [thing] for a cause to kill us:" for dár marḃaḋ: see Idiom 1): daɼ mo ḃriaṫar aɼ

PART IV.]   IDIOMS.   127

Naiṗi ní beᵹ liṅne ṗin uait, "'by my word,' says Naisi, 'we do not think that small from thee.'"

The two expressions iſ móṗ le and ní beaᵹ le (it is much with, it is not little with) are used to express the idea of unwillingness or grudging : iſ móṗ liom aon ṗinᵹín do taḃaiṗt dó, I think it much—I grudge—to give one penny to him : the very same idea is expressed by ní beaᵹ liom aon ṗinᵹín, &c., I think it not little—I grudge—one penny, I think one penny enough, &c. The two reverse expressions (ní móṗ le—iſ beaᵹ le) are used to express willingness—not grudging, &c.: ní móṗ liom na tṗí ba ſo do taḃaiṗt dó, I do not think it much—I am quite willing—I do not grudge—to give him these three cows; which might also be expressed by saying, iſ beaᵹ liom, &c.—I think it little—I would give more, I would have more, I would want more; I am willing—I do not grudge, &c.—do ḃeiṗmíd áṗ m-briaṫaṗ, aṗ ṗiad, nač beaᵹ linn a m-beuṗaṁ ᵹo Ḟionn díoḃ, "'we give our word,' said they ' we think it not small—we grudge—what (a = all that: see p. 47) we shall bring of them to Finn.'" (See Mr. Standish O'Grady's note, in the "Pursuit of Diarmaid and Grainne," p. 140.)

When móṗ and beaᵹ are used with the preposition do, they give the idea of enough or not enough for a person: níoṗ beaᵹ do (maṗḃaḋ ḃaṗ n-aiṫṗeač) maṗ eiṗic uaiḃṗe, (the killing of your fathers) is not small to him—is enough for him—should suffice for him—as an eric (fine) from you: níoṗ beaᵹ duit a ḃa do ḃṗeiṫ ó Ḟhionn, "it was not little for you—it was enough for you—to take away his cows from Finn."

29. Woe to.

Iſ maiṗᵹ don ḃ-ḟeaṗ ſin, woe to that man : a ṁaiṗᵹ do'n dṗunᵹ ᵹoiṗeaṗ do'n olc maiṫ, "woe to those who call evil good." Expressions of this kind are sometimes elliptical; as, iſ maiṗᵹ nač n-déanann coṁaiṗle ḃeaᵹ-ṁná, "woe [to him] who doeth not the counsel of a good wife " (lit. " it is woe who doeth not," &c.).

30. So .. as: as .. as.

When these "correspondent conjunctions" are expressed in Irish, the second one is usually translated either by aᵹuſ, "and," or by le, "with:" aᵹuſ a duḃaiṗt ṗia an tan do ḃiod a ṁac coṁ aṗṗačta aᵹuſ ᵹo líonṗad a ṁeuṗ an fod, "and he said to her when his son should be so grown (coṁ aṗṗačta) as that his finger would fill the ring" (lit.

"so grown *and* that his finger," &c.): do bí a ḟleaġ cóṁ pearṁap le mol muillinn, "his spear was as thick as the shaft of a mill" (lit. "as thick *with*.")

Aṡuṗ follows aṁlaiḋ or aiṅla (thus, so, in this manner), much in the same way as it follows cóṁ; and in this use it sometimes answers very nearly to "viz.:" aṗ aṁlaiḋ do ḟuaiṗ Naiṗi acaṗ Déiṗḋṗe, acaṗ an Ceannċaeṁ eṫappa, "it is thus he found Naisi and Déirdre, *and* the *Cenn-chaemh* (a kind of chess-board) between them.' (Meaning, "it was thus he found them, *viz.*, with the *Cenn-chaemh* between them.")

31. Every other day : every second day : every alternate day.

Phrases like these are often expressed in Irish by the indefinite pronoun ġaċ, followed by the preposition le or ṗe ġaċ le Ḋoṁnaċ aṡ ḋul ċum ṫeampoill, going to the church every other (or every alternate) Sunday: na ṫṗí ṗíġṫe ṗin do Ċhuataiḋ Dé Danann do bí i ḃ-ḟlaiṫioṗ Eiṗeann ṡaċ ṗe m-bliaġain, "these three kings of the Tuatha De Danann were in the sovereignty of Erin every other year" (i.e. each for a year).

32. The Head.

The word for *head* is used in Irish, as it is in most languages, in a great variety of idiomatic phrases. Some have been already noticed among the compound propositions; and these and others will be understood from the following examples. A ġ-ceann bliaḋna, at the end of a year: do bí ṗiaḋ a ġ-ceann na ṗaiṫċe, they were at the end of the field. A duḃaiṗṫ Naiṗi le h-Aṗḋan ḋul aiṗ ċeann Ḟeṗġuiṗ, "Naisi said to Ardan to go for Fergus" ("to go on the head of Fergus"): ṗillṗe aiṗ a ġ-ceann, "turn thou back for them" ("on their head"). O naċ liom ḋul ón ġ-conṫaḃaiṗṫ ṗo am ċeann, "since I am not able to escape from this danger [that lies] before me" (am ċeann, "in my head" = before me). Raċṗaḋ aḋ ċeann, a Ḟinn, aṡuṗ a ġ-ceann na Ḟéinne, "I will go to thee (or before thee), O Finn, and to the Feni" ("in thy head and in the head of the Feni"). Acaṗ beiṗiḋ buaiḋ acaṗ bennaċṫain bá ċenn, "and bear ye victory and blessing on its account" (ḋá ċenn, "from its head"). Ṫaṗ ċeann ṡuṗ ṗaoil an ṫoiṗċeaċ naċ ṗaiḋ baoġal aṗ biṫ aṗ ṗéin, "although the rich man thought that there was no danger at all to (i.e. of) himself" (ṫaṗ ċeann ṡuṗ, "over the head that" = although). Iṗ ionġna ḋuiṫṗe an ṡṗaḋ ṗin do tabairt bamra tar ceann Phinn, an Diarmaid, "'it is a wonder for thee to give that love to me instead of (to) Finn' says Diarmaid" (tar ceann Phinn, "over the head of Finn," in preference to Finn, instead of Finn)

33. A proper noun with the genitive of a noun of office.*

When a proper noun is followed by a noun in the genitive signifying a profession, office, trade, or calling, the resulting phrase has a curious idiomatic meaning.

Seaġan an ḟiġeadóra, which is word for word, "John of the weaver," means in reality "John (the son, son-in-law, servant, or some other close connection) of the weaver:" Seaġan na baintreabaiġe, "John (the son, &c.) of the widow."

If, while the proper name is in the nominative, the second noun is also in the nominative, the meaning is quite different, the second noun being then simply in apposition to the first: thus Ferġur maor (nom.) means "Fergus the steward;": but Ferġur an ṁaoir (gen.) is "Fergus (the son, &c.) of the steward."

Suppose, now, you have to express in Irish such a phrase as "the house of Fergus the steward," in which the proper name must be in the genitive: as the two nouns are in apposition, the second, according to a rule of Syntax (Rule 6, p. 96) should also be in the genitive: teaċ Fherġuir an ṁaoir. But here is an ambiguity; for, according to the present idiom, this expression would also mean "the house of Fergus (the son, &c.) of the steward." To avoid this ambiguity, a disagreement in case is allowed in such expressions, between the two nouns, when they are in apposition. Thus "the house of Fergus the steward" is teaċ Fherġuir maor (in which Fherġuir is gen. and maor nom.); whereas teaċ Fherġuir an ṁaoir is understood to mean "the house of Fergus (the son, &c.) of the steward." So in Dr. MacHale's translation of Homer, the first two lines are rendered:—

bruṫ Acuil ṗeinn, óiġ neaṁḋa, a'r buan ḟearġ;
Acuil mic Peil, an ġairġideaċ teinnteaċ ġarġ.

"The wrath of Achilles sing, O heavenly virgin, and his enduring anger, of Achilles son of Peleus, *the fiery fierce hero.*"

---

* The substance of this explanation and the illustrative examples have been taken from an interesting Essay on the present state of the Irish language in Munster, written and sent to the Royal Irish Academy by Mr. John Fleming of Rathgormuck.

Here the last noun ᵹɑıɼᵹıŏeɑċ, with its two adjectives, is in the nominative, while ɑ́cuıl, with which it is in apposition, is genitive.

In the first example, Rule 7, p. 96, beɑn Sheɑᵹɑın ɑn ꝼıᵹeɑŏóꞃɑ, accordingly, is not "the wife of John the weaver," but "the wife of John (son, &c.) of the weaver;" the wife of John the weaver, would be expressed by beɑn Sheɑᵹɑın ꝼıᵹeɑŏóıꞃ.

34. Possession.

There is no verb in Irish corresponding to the English verb "to have" as expressing possession; and the sentence "the man has a book," is expressed in Irish by the verb cá and the preposition ɑᵹ, in this form, cá leɑbɑꞃ ɑᵹ ɑn ŏuıne, "a book is at (or with) the man :" cɑ ɑıꞃᵹeɑŏ ɑᵹum (" money is with me"), I have money: cıɑ bé ɑᵹ ɑ b-ꝼuıl ɑıꞃᵹeɑŏ (" whoever with whom is money"), whoever has money. Ní ꝼéıŏıꞃ le ŏuıne ɑn nıŏ nɑċ m-beıŏeɑŏ ɑıᵹe ŏo cɑbɑıꞃc uɑıŏ, ɑᵹuꞃ ní b-ꝼuıl ŏo-ṁɑꞃbċɑċc ɑᵹumꞃɑ. "it is impossible for a man to give away what he does not himself possess, and I do not possess immortality" (word-for-word: "it is not possible for a man the thing which would not be with him to give from him, and not is immortality with myself"). Ŏo uıᵹel Conċubɑꞃ bonɑċ ɑcɑꞃ ŏo ꝼıɑꝼꞃɑıᵹ ŏé ɑn ꞃɑıŏ ꝼleŏ ollɑṁ ɑıᵹe ŏo, "Conchobhar addressed Borach and inquired of him whether he had a feast prepared for him" (lit. : "whether a feast was ready with him [i.e. Borach] for him [i.e. Conchobar."]

The use of pronouns in this idiom sometimes gives rise to further idiomatic complications. Cıɑ ɑᵹuınne ɑᵹ ɑ b-ꝼuıl ɑn ꝼıꞃınne? "Which of us has the truth?" This is word for word: "Which of us with whom is the truth?" and the interrogative appears without any government or other syntactical connection. Some good authorities believe that the preposition ɑᵹ in this construction governs not only the relative ɑ, but also, by a sort of attraction, the interrogative cıɑ. Cá beɑn eıle ɑ n-Coċɑıll ɑ b-ꝼuıl ɑıcı coꞃóın ɑıꞃ, "there is another woman in Youghal who has a crown on him" (i.e. to whom he owes a crown : Idiom 16). Here, also, there is an apparent redundancy, the act of "having" being expressed doubly, namely, both by the relative ɑ before b-ꝼuıl, and by ɑıcı; and the relative, according to the same authority, would be governed by the preposition ɑᵹ of ɑıcı. The sentence may be expressed without redundancy in this manner :—Cá beɑn eile a n-Eocaill ag a b-puil copóin aip. The last example exactly resembles the English "there is a man in Dublin whom I owe a pound to him:" and perhaps it would be better to consider it, like the English sentence, merely as bad grammar, which is to be avoided by using a different form of expression in the manner shown. The apparent redundancy of the first example, which is from a good authority, cannot, however, be got rid of in this way. So also in, cia leip an ceac pin (who owns that house), the le of leip would appear to govern the pronoun with which it is combined, and also the interrogative cia.

35. Ownership.

Ownership is expressed by the verb ip and the preposition le, with: ip leacpa an ceac, "the house belongs to thee" (lit. "it is with thee the house"): ip lem' acaip na ba pin, those cows belong to my father ("it is with my father those cows'): cia léip na ba pin, who owns those cows? ("who with him [are] those cows?") Oip ip le neac éigin do Chuaca De Danann na muca, "for the pigs belong to some person of the Tuatha De Danann." (A wizard holds a golden branch in his hand, and king Cormac asks him) an leac péin an cpaob pin? "Does that branch belong to thyself?"

Observe the distinction between this idiom and the last in the following sentence:—Ta aipgead go leóp agad, acc ní leac péin é, "thou hast plenty of money, but it does not belong to thyself."

36. Wanting a thing.

The idea of wanting a thing, including a wish to get it, is usually expressed by the verb cá and the preposition ó from: ca leabap uaim, I want a book: lit., "a book is from me:" cpeud acá uaic? "What dost thou want?"

37. Genitive plurals of Personal Pronouns.

Each of the three prepositional pronouns, againn, agaib, aca, has two different meanings, which are always easily distinguished by the context.

1. Possession, as in Idiom 34: Do bí leabaip aca, they had books.

2. The sense of a genitive plural when following words denoting a part: gac peap aguinn, "each man *of us;*" po eipig an dapa peap acopan do béanam an cleapa, "the

second man *of them* (acoṗan, "of themselves") arose to perform the feat:" cia aguinne ag a ḃ-ḟuil an ḟiṗinne, aṗ Ḟionn, "'which *of us* has the truth,' says Finn" (ag a ḃ-ḟuil, "with whom is" = " has :" see Idiom 34).

38. To give a name.

To give a name to a thing is often expressed in Irish by *to put a name on it* : maṗ go ccugeaṗ ḃá ḃancuaṫaḋ aiṗ ḃheċoill agur aiṗ Ḋhanann, "as (the name) 'two ladies' was put on Bechoill and Danann : i.e. as they "were called 'two ladies.'" Maṗ go ḃ-cug cleaṗ aiṗ an g-cleaṗ ṗin, "as he called that feat 'a feat :'" (lit. "as that he put [the name] 'feat' on that feat").

Sometimes, also, to give such and such a name to a thing is expressed by " to say such and such a name with a thing :" Ror-ḃá-ṡáileaḋ ṗiṗ a ṗáiḋṫeaṗ Luimneaċ aniu, "Ros-dashaileach which is called Limerick now" (lit. " R. with which is said 'Limerick' now").

39. Ḋe after comparatives.

The prepositional pronoun ḃe "of it," is often postfixed to comparatives, giving rise to some idiomatic phrases. Agur gion go ḃ-ḟuil cuiḋ aguinn ḃo ṁaṗḃaḋ Ḋiaṗmaḋa, ní móiḋe ḃo ġeuḃaḋ (Aongur) an ḟiṗinne uaim, "and although we have no part in killing Diarmaid, Aongus would not *the more* receive the truth from us" (here móiḋe is ḃe added to mó, the comparative of móṗ, great : for gion go = "although not :" see Idiom 11). Ir ruṗaiḋe ḋ'Ḟhionn áṗ loṗgna leanaṁain, an eaċṗa ḃeiṫ againn, "it is the easier for Finn to follow our track that we have the horses" (ruṗaiḋe = ḃe after ruṗa, comparative of ruṗur, easy): i.e. "our having the horses makes it easier for Finn," &c.

40. " A man of great strength."

"A man of great strength," is expressed by the Irish ṗeaṗ ir móṗ neaṗc, which translated word for word is "a man (who) is great strength :" the words móṗ neaṗc being in the nominative, and not in the genitive, as might be expected from the English "*of* great strength." This idiom is extremely common in Irish, the verb ir in some of its forms being always used ; and when translating it, remember that the Irish words, though in the nominative case, convey the exact sense of the genitive with " of " in English, and must be rendered accordingly. Ní paıb a g-cómaimṗıṙ ṗıṙ ḟeaṙ ba ṁó ón aguṙ aıṙgeab ınd Dıaṙmaıd, "there was not at the same time with him a man who had more gold and silver than Diarmaid" (lit. "a man [who] was greater gold and silver," i.e. "a man who was *of* greater gold and silver.") Do beaṙcaṙ an beıṫ ba ṁaṁda cṙuṫ, "I saw a lady (of) bright shape:" Talaṁ ba ḟeáṙṙ bıab aguṙ beoċ, "a land (of) the best food and drink:" Oıṙín ba ṫṙeun neaṙṫ a'ṙ luṫ, "Oisin of mighty strength and vigour."

Sometimes the preposition go (with) is used instead of the verb: as ḟeaṙ go mór neaṙṫ, a man *with* great strength, i.e. a man of great strength.

41. A wish.

"I wish I had such and such a thing," is often expressed in Irish by some such form of phrase as "Alas that I have not got it!" the word gan being generally used as the negative particle. Aṙ ṫṙuaıg gan peaca 'n ṁaoıṙ agum! "I wish I had the shepherd's pet!" (Here aṙ ṫṙuaıg, "it is pity" = "alas:" agum is used to denote possession, with its verb understood—Idiom 34: and the word-for-word translation is "it is pity not the pet of the shepherd with me." A Dhıa gan mé am' aḃaıllín, "I wish I were an apple" ("O God, I not an apple"—or "in my apple.")

42. One noun asserted of another by tá.

When one noun is asserted of another (or of a pronoun) by the verb tá, in any of its forms, it requires the aid of the preposition a or ann, "in," and of one of the possessive pronouns, giving rise to a unique and extremely curious idiom. Thus "I am a man," if expressed in Irish by tá, will be (not tá mé ḟeaṙ, but) tá mé am' ḟeaṙ, which is word for word, "I am in my man." Bí ṫúṙa ab' ṙgían aguṙ mıṙe am ḟeoıl, "be thou the knife and I the flesh." (lit. "be thou in thy knife and I in my flesh"). Beċoıll aguṙ Danann bo bí ı n-a m-baınṫígeaṙnaıb, "Bechoill and Danann who were princesses" ("who were in their princesses"): ıṙ ḟeáṙṙ éıṙean míle uaıṙ ná ṫuṙa, cuıṙ a g-cáṙ go b-ḟuıl tú ab' ṙıg no ab' ṗṙıonnṙa. "he is better a thousand times than thou, even supposing that thou art a king or a prince" (cuıṙ a g-cáṙ, "put in case" = "suppose" or "although"): ṗagaıb na baoıne báṙ cuıb aca 'n-a n-ógánaıb, aġuſ cuıb aca 'n-a ſeanóıpıġıb, "men die ('receive death:' Idiom 3), "some of them (cuıb aca: Idiom 37) as youths, and some as old men" ("some of them in their youths and some of them in their old men.") A Ḋhıa, ġan mé am aḃaıllín!" "would God that I were an apple!" ("O God without me in my apple!").

Even when one thing is not directly asserted of another, this use of the preposition and the possessive is extremely common in Irish. Táımſe am' ċobla, "I am asleep" ("I am in my sleep"): b'éıpıġ ına ſeaſam, "he stood up" ("he arose in his standing"): mıſe am' aonap, "myself alone" ("myself in my one person"): clanna Lıp ına ġ-ceaṫpap, (the four children of Lir) ("the children of Lir in their four-persons").

The preposition ann is used with tá without any governed noun, to denote existence in general; as atá aon Ḋıa amáın ann, there is only one God; here the ann in the end, which has no representative in the translation, means "in it," i. e. in existence. Sometimes this ann answers very nearly to the English "here," or "there;" as ıſ tú atá ann "it is thou who art in it—who art in existence—who art there."

43. Differences between ıſ and tá.

There are several differences, as to the manner of application, between ıſ and tá.

1. Iſ is a simple copula, and is used to predicate one thing of another, or to connect an attribute with its subject; as ıſ mé an t-ſlıġe, an ſíſınne, aġuſ an ḃeaṫa, "I am the way, the truth, and the life."

But if existence in connection with place is to be predicated of the subject, tá is used; as tá mé a m-baıle ata clıaṫ, I am in Dublin: an paıb tú ann ſın? wert thou there?

If an adjective is to be predicated of a noun, either ıſ or tá may be used:—ıſ bſeaġ an lá é, or tá an lá bſeaġ, "it is a fine day," or "the day is fine."

2. Iſ connects one noun or pronoun with another, as predicate and subject directly, and without the aid of any other word; as ıſ ſeap mé, I am a man. But tá cannot do this without the aid of the preposition ı or ınn and the possessive pronoun, as already explained in last Idiom; as tá mé am' ſeap, I am a man ("I am in my man.")

3. Iꞃ expresses simply that a person or thing is **so**, and implies nothing more. But when the assertion is made by cá, there is *often* something more implied than is contained in the direct assertion—the idea that the person or thing has not always been so—has come to be so, &c. Thus, if you say to me iꞃ ꞃeaꞃ é, your assertion means nothing more than that "he is a man"—not a woman or a coward, &c. If we see a figure approach in the dark, and that after looking close you find it is a man, your correct phraseology is, iꞃ ꞃeaꞃ é, by which I understand you to mean "it is a man"—not a woman, or a beast, or a ghost.

But if you say to me ca ꞃé 'n-a ꞃeaꞃ ("he is in his man"), here I take you to mean a very different thing—that he is now a man, no longer a boy, grown up to be a man. If I were speaking of a person as if he were a mere boy, and that you wished to correct this false impression, the proper phraseology would be, ca ꞃé 'n-a ꞃeaꞃ.

But though this idea of an implied change is often contained in an assertion made by cá, it is not always so; as ní ḃ-ꝼuil acc aon Ḋia aṁáin ann, aca 'n-a ꞃioꞃ-ꞃꞃioꞃaiḋ, there is only one God alone, who is a pure spirit: here the last assertion is made by cá though there can be no change.

4. Cá is used with aᵹ to denote possession (Idiom 43); iꞃ is used with le to denote ownership (Idiom 44); in these two applications the two verbs cannot change places.

Cá may indeed be used with le, but the idea conveyed is not "belonging to," but "being favourable to:" Ḋo ḃí Ꞃolup leo "(Eolus was with them"), does not mean that they were the owners of Eolus (which would be the meaning if iꞃ had been used), but that "Eolus was favourable to them"—"was on their side."

5. Cá is used with the Irish words for cold, heat, hunger, &c., as in Idiom 36; as cá ocꞃaꞃ oꞃm, hunger is in me, I am hungry: here iꞃ canno' be used.

6. When the comparative of an adjective is used as in the following sentences, either verb will answer :—iꞃ ꞃaiḋḃꞃe é ná miꞃe or cá ꞃé nioꞃ ꞃaiḋḃꞃe ná miꞃe, he is richer than I.

But when the superlative is employed, iꞃ, not cá, must be used:—iꞃ é iꞃ ꞃeaꞃ iꞃ ꞃaiḋḃꞃe ꞃan ḋúicce é, he is the richest man in the country.

APPENDIX.

Additional Examples of Declensions.

FIRST DECLENSION.
breac, *a trout.*

	Singular.	Plural.
N.	breac.	bric.
G.	bric.	breac.
D.	breac.	breacaib.
V.	a bric.	a breaca.

SECOND DECLENSION.
Cor, *a foot.*

N.	cor.	cora.
G.	coire	cor.
D.	coir.	coraib.

THIRD DECLENSION.
Pigeadóir, *a weaver; masc.*

N.	pigeadóir.	pigeadóirige.
G.	pigeadóra.	pigeadóir
D.	pigeadóir.	pigeadóirib.

Ataír, *a father; masc.*

N.	ataír.	aitre, aitreaca.
G.	atar.	aitreac.
D.	ataír.	aitreacaib.

(Mátair, a mother, and brátair or dearbrátair, a brother, are declined in the same way.)

bliadain, *a year; fem.*

N.	bliadain.	bliadanta.
G.	bliadna.	bliadan.
D.	bliadain	bliadantaib.

Ainm, *a name.*

N.	ainm.	anmanna.
G.	ainme, anma.	anmann.
D.	ainm	anmannaib.

FOURTH DECLENSION.
Teine, *a fire.*

	Singular.	Plural.
N.	teine.	teinte
G.	teine.	teinead.
D.	teine.	teintib.

Éinín, *a little bird.*

N.	éinín.	éinínibe.
G.	éinín.	éinín.
D.	éinín.	éinínib.

FIFTH DECLENSION.
Lánama, *a married couple.*

N.	lánama.	lánamna.
G.	lánaman.	lánaman.
D.	lánamain.	lánamnaib.

IRREGULAR NOUNS.
Ga, *a spear.*

N.	ga, gat.	gaoi, gaeta, gaoite.
G.	gai, gaoi.	gat, gaetad, gaoitead.
D.	ga, gai.	gaoib, geatail gaoitib.

Cró, *a hut, a sheepfold.*

N.	cró.	craoite, cróite
G.	cró.	cró.
D.	cró.	craoitib, cróitib.
V.	a cro.	a craoite, a cróite.

Sliab, *a mountain.*

N.	sliab.	sléibte
G.	sléibe.	sléibtead.
D.	sliab.	sléibtib.

BIBLIOLIFE

Old Books Deserve a New Life
www.bibliolife.com

Did you know that you can get most of our titles in our trademark **EasyScript**™ print format? **EasyScript**™ provides readers with a larger than average typeface, for a reading experience that's easier on the eyes.

Did you know that we have an ever-growing collection of books in many languages?

Order online:
www.bibliolife.com/store

Or to exclusively browse our **EasyScript**™ collection:
www.bibliogrande.com

At BiblioLife, we aim to make knowledge more accessible by making thousands of titles available to you – quickly and affordably.

Contact us:
BiblioLife
PO Box 21206
Charleston, SC 29413

Made in the USA
San Bernardino, CA
27 May 2014